D0387927

CHILDREN'S MINISTRY GUIDE *for* SMALLER CHURCHES

by Rick Chromey

Group

Loveland, Colorado

....

DEDICATION

To my grandparents, Ray and Barbara Stingley.
How can I say thanks?
You raised a "David" to rout giants.
I love you.

Children's Ministry Guide for Smaller Churches

Copyright © 1995 Rick Chromey

Credits

Book Acquisitions Editor: Mike Nappa
Editor: Beth Rowland Wolf
Senior Editor: Paul Woods
Creative Products Director: Joani Schultz
Copy Editor: Amy Simpson
Art Director: Lisa Chandler
Cover Art Director: Liz Howe
Cover Designer: Tricia McCusker
Designer: Joel Armstrong
Computer Graphic Artist: Rosalie Lawrence
Cover Illustrator: Sam Thiewes
Cartoonists: John Duckworth, Randy Glasbergen, Doug Hall, John McPherson, Rob Portlock, and Ron Wheeler
Production Manager: Gingar Kunkel

Unless otherwise noted, Scriptures quoted from The Youth Bible, New Century Version, copyright © 1991 by Word Publishing, Dallas, Texas 75039. Used by permission.

Library of Congress Cataloging-in-Publication Data

Chromey, Rick.
    Children's ministry guide for smaller churches / by Rick Chromey.
      p. cm.
    ISBN 1-55945-600-0
    1. Church work with children—United States. 2. Small churches—United States. I. Title.
BV639.C4C47 1995   95-35065
259'.22—dc20   CIP

10 9 8 7 6 5 4 3 2 1   04 03 02 01 00 99 98 97 96 95
Printed in the United States of America.

ACKNOWLEDGMENTS

Writing a book is hardly a solo venture. It's the product of years of encouragement, education, and experience, not to mention hours of the three R's: research, 'riting, and revision. The following people contributed to this work.

● First and foremost, Patti, Becca, and Ryan. Thanks for letting me live at the office and for reading the rough drafts. (Patti, your insights were great!) I promise we'll be a "family" now. I love you.

● Beth Rowland Wolf and Mike Nappa, my editors. Beth, I learned volumes from your red marks. You pushed me to excel...thanks. Mike, from the beginning you believed in this work. Thanks for making the dream come true.

● The small-church pastors, teachers, children's leaders, youth ministers, elders, deacons, and Sunday school superintendents who contributed their time and ideas in two national surveys. Pastors and children's workers from a wide variety of denominations participated in the surveys. Some of the children's workers who participated in the survey are from churches that are very small (10 to 15 members). Others are from congregations moving out of the small-church arena. They are the mustard seeds who are changing the world. This is *their* book.

● Members of my home church in Lewistown, Montana. Your love and encouragement to an often misguided boy have forged an unshakable faith. Thanks to Ron and Lois, Margaret, Dave and Arla, Ed, Donna, and other unsung saints.

● George Barna—I would be remiss to pass over his influential work. From *User Friendly Churches* to his recent *Turn-Around Churches,* Barna is a leader in church research and growth tactics. His thorough surveys of American congregational life are a vital tool in understanding where the church is now and where it's heading.

● My special friends and congregations. These include the faculty, staff, and students at Boise Bible College; Andy Hansen; Christ in Youth, Inc.; David Hennig; Dan Cravatt; Dr. Eleanor Daniel; Don Raymond and Wallula Christian

Church (Leavenworth, Kansas); Kirkwood Road Christian Church (Kirkwood, Missouri); and State College Christian Church (State College, Pennsylvania). You always believed, even when I didn't.

● Finally, those who created a writer: Ann Rapkoch, Dave Byerly, Dr. Richard Brown, Dana Eynon, Sam Stone, and Thom Schultz. You taught me how and gave me opportunity. "Thank-you" will never completely express my gratitude.

Rick Chromey

CONTENTS

INTRODUCTION   7

Chapter One
SMALL ADVANTAGES   13

Chapter Two
GETTING FOCUSED   21

Chapter Three
SMALL SUCCESSES   33

Chapter Four
BALANCED MINISTRY   45

Chapter Five
FINDING HELP   59

Chapter Six
FINDING MONEY   75

Chapter Seven
TEACHING TO PRODUCE LEARNING   87

Chapter Eight
EFFECTIVE PROGRAMS   103

Chapter Nine
CHILDREN AND WORSHIP   115

Chapter Ten
REACHING OUT   127

RECOMMENDED RESOURCES   137

INTRODUCTION

"The kingdom of heaven is like a mustard seed that a man planted in his field. That seed is the smallest of all seeds, but when it grows, it is one of the largest garden plants. It becomes big enough for the wild birds to come and build nests in its branches"

(Matthew 13:31b-32).

In the heart of Montana, a church of 90 members lies miles and miles from opportunity, popular resources, and innovative curriculum. Money has never been an issue because there isn't any. No children's minister, save a summer intern or two, has ever graced the staff. And there are no stunning facilities, playgrounds, or gymnasiums.

In almost every way, this small congregation is average. The Sunday school teachers, who have little training, nurture their charges in an educational philosophy rooted in tradition and pride. For example, one woman faithfully taught the junior girls class for nearly 40 years. This recently retired saint kept on the classroom wall a list of the names of the girls she taught. Her success was indicated by the stars pasted next to the names of former students who now profess Christianity.

Smaller churches, though often overlooked in this age of "big is better," are remarkable in their accomplishments. In fact, this Montana congregation has changed the world—literally.

In the last 20 years, this seemingly insignificant congregation has sent nearly two dozen of its own into full-time Christian ministry across the nation and beyond. Among them are preachers, missionaries, people who work with the hearing impaired, musicians, children's pastors, and Bible-college professors. And dozens of churches across the nation are blessed with the lay leadership of men and women who grew up in this church.

I'm proud of the congregation in Montana. It's my home church. And like many churches, this one is a "mustard seed." It is a tiny kernel in budgets and buildings but a towering tree in influence and inspiration.

The Exciting Faith of Children

Smaller churches are exciting places for ministry. I believe that a dynamic children's ministry is often what makes a smaller church successful. Successes (or failures) in children's ministry will determine who is in the congregation a generation from now.

We need to use our resources to instill exciting faith in kids. An exciting faith doesn't come by chance, and neither does apathy. Most apathetic teens have grown disinterested because of their church experiences as children. If we spent more time and money creating exciting children's ministries, perhaps the excitement would carry over into the teen years.

Children are the church of tomorrow, but they're also

part of the church of *today.* Children can worship and praise God *now.* Kids can serve in valuable ministry roles *now.* They can encourage and support other church members *now.* And while larger churches may have more money to finance creative programs for children, often the smaller churches possess greater opportunities to challenge the kids to be active parts of the body.

When was the last time you saw children actively involved, week in and week out, in a larger church? It rarely happens. But the smaller church can provide opportunities for children to lead. This book will give you dozens of ideas on how to involve children in ministry.

The Smaller Church

People in smaller churches often feel outnumbered by those in larger, more dynamic churches. But according to current church demographics, the average congregation has a membership of about 160 people. On a Sunday morning, between 75 and 125 come to worship. This book is for those who work with children in churches of 150 or fewer members.

Research shows that as a children's worker in a smaller church, you probably fit one of these four descriptions:

Judy, who has no formal ministry credentials, is a lay volunteer in an Ohio church. Lack of time and money keep her from attending helpful ministry workshops. The church helps all it can, but few new ideas fly in this town of 900. Faithfulness and a love for children motivate Judy to stick with her ministry. But she longs for creative helps—ministry ideas that will really work in her church of 60 members.

Mustard-Seed Faith

According to the Barna Research Group, the average church in America has

- 159 members,
- 102 people at a normal weekend worship service,
- 30 adults and 32 youth in Sunday school,
- one full-time staff person, and
- a median annual church budget of $82,000 (of which $32,000 is the senior pastor's compensation package).

Barna also surveyed unchurched people and found that 60 percent preferred a church made up of "under 200 people."[1]

Jim is a pastor at a white clapboard church of 125 members in rural Oregon. He doesn't have a lot of time for children's ministry, but he's young and the church is convinced that Jim can overhaul the program. Jim studied preaching at seminary, and he doesn't have a clue as to what children need.

Then there's Joan. She's a part-time, paid youth worker in Southern California. She works a 40-hour week in a coffee shop, then she gives another 20 hours to the children and teenagers in her congregation. It's not easy, and though she has a few children's ministry seminars under her belt, Joan feels far from adequate. She wants to do more.

Finally there's Mark, a full-time, paid Christian education minister. He works in a church of 125 members on the outskirts of St. Louis. Children's ministry is of great interest to him, but his job description includes ministry to all age groups, including teenagers and adults. Mark has books packed with games and lessons, but what he wants is a

DUCKWORTH

framework. He's looking for workable strategies, and they've got to be good stuff that won't tax his time, people, or budget.

Regardless of where you fit in the mix, the ideas in this book will provide you with options for smaller-church children's ministry. Every church is unique. You may need to bounce these ideas off your own denominational structures, your own ministry philosophy, and your own congregation's needs. But don't be afraid to risk trying what you read about. An idea that sounds outrageous may spark success in your children's ministry.

This book offers a vision of hope. If a church of 90 in Lewistown, Montana, can impact the world, a smaller congregation in Drain, Oregon—or Madison, Wisconsin; Canadian, Texas; New Richmond, Ohio; or even your hometown—can too.

....

1. George Barna, "Understanding Ministry in a Changing Culture" Notebook (Barna Research Group, 1994), 26, 108.

Chapter One

SMALL ADVANTAGES

*"Each of you
has received a gift
to use to serve others.
Be good servants
of God's various gifts
of grace"*
(1 Peter 4:10).

To be small is to be blessed, especially in children's ministry. Most educators now believe that the *smaller* the classroom, the better the learning. Personal, individual instruction is more conducive to learning than instruction in large classes where some children can get lost in the shuffle.

You can build a powerful children's ministry on the strengths of a smaller church. Let's look at five specific advantages of small-church children's ministry.

The Exciting Faith of a Child

I love the faith of children. It's can-do faith. Children have an innocent enthusiasm that inspires others. Children remind us of the way we used to be: carefree, exuberant, and unconcerned about failures.

Church researcher George Barna comments, "As adults, we have a tendency to memorialize things in programs and routines, frequently removing the spontaneity and enthusiasm from the activity."[1] Children can remind us of what's important. They enable adults to understand that faith need not be stale and static, but can be dynamic and full of wonder. That faith is action as well as belief. The following story shows what kids can do.

Carlos and Juanita were two kids who never missed Sunday school in their small church just north of the border between Texas and Mexico. For decades, the church had conducted "business as usual."

One Sunday, as the pastor preached about personal sacrifice and giving to others, Juanita had an idea: Wouldn't it be great to give Bibles to people across the border? After church, Juanita sold Carlos on the idea, and later her mother and father.

A Bible cost only 50 cents. Juanita set a goal of 100 Bibles, but $50 might as well have been $50,000 for this church of 25. Even so, Juanita and Carlos made the first contribution: $5 each they got from collecting and selling aluminum cans. The children created a "money Bible," which was passed around the church every week. At first, the offerings were as tiny as the church—a quarter here, a roll of pennies there.

But as the pennies added up, the congregation grew excited about the project. The women of the church held a bake sale to earn the remaining money. When the goal was reached, the Bibles were quickly purchased and the trip was planned. One hot July day, Juanita and Carlos rode into Mexico with their parents and the pastor to give away Bibles.

Within 20 minutes, all the Bibles were gone.

The experience excited Juanita and Carlos. The next time they raised $100, then $300, then over $500! More church members got behind the project. One family sold its television. Another man canceled his newspaper subscription. A men's group organized a "window wash" for local businesses. People held yard sales. And several members committed to passing out Bibles.

"We realize that our church camp isn't the fanciest place, but let's try to make the best of it! Whoever goes home with the most bug bites gets to come back next year for free!"

Hundreds of lives have been changed in Mexico and in this small Texas church. And it began with the vision of two children, ages 6 and 7.

Any children's ministry should begin by encouraging the active faith of children.

The smaller church can open doors for children to live out their faith exuberantly. In larger churches, so many adults are available for ministry that children rarely have the opportunity to express their faith.

In a smaller church, children naturally take a more active role. It's not uncommon in a small church for a child to stand up during prayer request time and ask the congregation to pray about a loose tooth. Children feel free to respond aloud to the pastor's rhetorical questions. They're encouraged to give announcements, to sing, and to serve alongside the adults. Smaller churches give children opportunities to express their faith actively.

Potential for Persuading Parents

A strong children's ministry can attract adults to your church.

Two years ago, Jim's 9-year-old daughter begged him and his wife to attend a vacation Bible school closing program. At first he balked, mostly because he remembered church as boring, and his daughter's program was at the same small, "boring" church Jim had attended as a child. Jim gave in to his daughter's pleas and attended the program. He hasn't missed a Sunday since.

What persuaded Jim to return to church? He was influenced by the genuine love the teachers showed for his daughter, and he was impressed by the quality and quantity of children's programming. A dynamic church ministry to children will almost always attract young families.

A smaller church can capitalize on this opportunity. In a small church, both children and adults can involve themselves in groups where they feel emotionally secure, appreciated, and respected. Another advantage is that because small-church leaders tend to know the children better, programs can be carried out on a more personal basis. Finally, individual opportunity is greater. For example, one-to-one instruction is more possible due to smaller class size. When we build programs for the individuals in our church, people are more likely to feel a sense of belonging and will be more likely to stay and to grow spiritually.

A Close Family of Believers

Children have more contact with adults in smaller churches, and adults are familiar with almost every child. Children who see God's love and a deep faith in adults they admire will be affected for eternity. In the small church it's easy to include children in church life.

As a boy, I had 90 parents and grandparents, aunts and uncles, brothers and sisters! I was on a first-name basis with almost every adult in the church. "Grandma" Lois and "Grandpa" Ron held me in the hospital right after I was born. "Mom and Dad" Olson took me camping. "Uncle" Jim taught me to draw fish. "Aunt" Margaret gave me a job.

I grew up among adults. I sang with adults in the choir. I was always a welcome member of their Bible Tick-Tack-Toe teams. I helped build our church building. I participated in Wednesday night Bible studies. I washed countless communion cups and folded a bottomless box of bulletins. And in every single activity I was alongside an adult.

The children in a smaller church can benefit from close, personal contact with adults. Children should be welcomed to join almost every adult activity, whether it's a fellowship meal or a fishing adventure.

Children Today, Church Leaders Tomorrow

The smaller church can develop better leaders. Why? Because the smaller the congregation, the greater the opportunity for children to be active *leaders.*

Unfortunately, children are seldom allowed much participation with adults. Why? Because kids are unpredictable. They might mess up. They're too loud. Or not loud enough. They're unprofessional.

But when children are left out of church life, the message they hear is that they don't belong. Adults will lead adults, and certain adults will keep the kids out of the adults' hair.

Sometimes children are granted the privilege of attending "adult" worship, where they're expected to sit quietly and still so the adults can worship. They're given occasional opportunities to share a song, a puppet play, or a dramatic skit. But such opportunities are few, and children don't learn how to really serve and be a part of the church body.

The good news is that in the smaller church it's easy to do things differently. Children can have a place in leadership. They have closer relationships with adults, who can disciple them in the faith. Children can serve the smaller church in many ways. They can advance a slide projector, play a music soundtrack, pray for the offering, give a congregational announcement, or even help lead a song service.

You'll rarely see children doing such things in a larger church. The small congregation that often hurts for volunteers anyway has a great opportunity to really involve children. Children need not wait until they're 18 to be part of the church body. And if the smaller church creatively involves its children, those children will be more likely to stay in the church as they grow up.

Creative Ground for New Ideas

Of all age groups, children probably welcome new situations best—they love novelty and spontaneity. Barna asserts that the benefit of testing new programs with children is "the assurance that kids [will] provide honest feedback, enabling the church leaders to sharpen or forget about the program or communication."[2]

What types of ideas might a church "test" on its children? Churches can try innovative schedules for Sunday morning, creative teaching methods, or new worship songs. I know of a small church that struggled with a new computer system. The computer collected dust until the fourth-graders discovered it. They not only used it to play computer games, but also helped the adults learn to use it to organize and administrate church programs.

Few larger churches are going to allow a 9-year-old boy to play on its church computer, suggest potential new music for Sunday's worship, or give input on an innovative program. Once again, the smaller church has the edge. Giving children a significant role in the congregation is easier because children are more visible in the small church.

Furthermore, it's much easier to be flexible and spontaneous with 15 children than with 50. In large churches, the organization can grow to be so big that size prevents it from enjoying much liberty. Small churches can change quickly to respond to the needs of the children and the rest of the congregation. Small churches can change meeting times or program agendas much more quickly than a larger church can because communication lines are more direct.

Some may conclude that since children's ministry in a smaller church is more flexible, it should operate with little planning. They may think that "winging it" will better meet the needs of kids. Why plan at all, especially if you can change on a dime?

The answer is simple: Careful, thoughtful planning actually allows the children's worker to be more spontaneous. The goal is defined, the needs are assessed, and the resources are accounted for. The children's worker can creatively match needs and resources to create an efficient, exciting program that builds faith in children. And all of this work is done upfront—it's planning. If the needs change in the middle of the program, the children's worker will be able to change the program because he or she knows what resources are available.

An effective children's ministry within the smaller church will capitalize on the strengths of being small. Leaders will discipline themselves to plan programs, yet will reserve the right to change them. Such a ministry will involve children in developing programs that will affect the entire church body. The church will begin to see children as part of the congregation of *today,* not just tomorrow.

----

1. George Barna, *User Friendly Churches* (Ventura, CA: Regal Books, 1991), 124.

2. Barna, *User Friendly Churches,* 124.

Chapter Two

GETTING FOCUSED

"I went to Jerusalem and stayed there three days. Then at night I started out with a few men…I went up the valley at night, inspecting the wall. Then I said to them, 'You can see the trouble we have here. Jerusalem is a pile of ruins…Come, let's rebuild the wall of Jerusalem' "

(Nehemiah 2:11-12a, 15a, 17a).

A s a cupbearer to King Artaxerxes, Nehemiah was in a comfortable, secure leadership position. But when he heard that Jerusalem's walls were in ruins, Nehemiah was moved to tears and got permission to lead the rebuilding. Before doing so, however, he carefully evaluated the situation so the workers could focus their efforts where they were most needed.

Just as Nehemiah realized the advantages of effective evaluation, so should the leader of a smaller-church children's ministry. Nehemiah walked the entire perimeter of the wall, inspecting each crack and crevice. The leader of a smaller-church children's ministry should also survey the entire program to determine strengths and weaknesses and to know where to concentrate efforts.

Your evaluation should cover every aspect of your current ministry: curriculum, teachers, results, the learner's experience, facilities, equipment, and how the program is organized and administrated. You should also evaluate the needs of your church's children and the needs of your neighborhood's children. That way you can plan effective strategies for reaching out into the community.

Your evaluation may reveal resources you don't know about. You may find adults who are eager to begin a drama or puppet ministry, or older adults who long for contact with young children. You may find equipment, stage props, or teaching materials long forgotten in storage. Any of these could help you start a new ministry to children that will excite your entire congregation.

A thorough evaluation may also reveal programs that need to be drastically changed or even dropped. Dropping or revamping a program may at first be discouraging to the leaders involved. Those people, however, can then pour their energy into more effective programs and can have a greater impact on the lives of the children.

Evaluation also reveals what you're doing right. You might discover that your curriculum plan is meeting needs and building biblical knowledge in the lives of children. Or that you've got well-trained, gifted teachers and leaders. You may find that a program is doing an excellent job of attracting new families to your church. Evaluation affirms you for your successes and allows you to build on programs that are working.

A final advantage is that evaluation allows those in children's ministry to better plan for the future. When you know exactly how things are going in your ministry, you'll be able to compare your present program to the needs of the congregation and the community. Evaluation helps a smaller-church children's ministry look forward. The more comprehensive that evaluation is, the better your chance for future success.

Why Churches Don't Evaluate

Unfortunately, few small churches concern themselves with the future. Many believe that to look forward wastes energy best used to meet today's needs. To those people, evaluating and planning indicate a lack of trust in God. One small-church leader told me, "Jesus said not to worry about tomorrow." We should, of course, obey Jesus' command, but planning *isn't* "worrying." Jesus also said that if one wants to build a tower, he must first sit down and estimate the cost (Luke 14:28). Through evaluation and planning, a smaller church counts the cost of effective, life-changing ministry.

So why don't smaller churches evaluate their ministry to children?

● **Time**—Proper evaluation takes time, and because smaller-church children's workers already wear many hats, evaluation can eat up time that seems better invested elsewhere. Evaluation is invaluable, though. Many problems don't show themselves for years. Without proper evaluation, an ineffective program can go on for years before anyone notices it.

Almost every small congregation I surveyed had evaluated its programs, but much of the evaluation done in small churches doesn't ask enough tough questions. My survey also suggested that the smaller the church, the less accurate the evaluation. Members of small churches are more connected, so evaluation is usually informal and confined to conversations over coffee. While such informal evaluations can be beneficial, they rarely result in long-term change. Formal evaluations carry more weight in making positive change in ministry.

After gathering information, every church must make decisions about changes in policy, changes in staffing, and

"The Lord caused me to lie down in green pastures once, and I got in big trouble for getting grass stains on my good clothes."

the realignment of resources. The task can seem insurmountable, but the time taken to seriously evaluate and make changes in your ministry will be time well spent. It will make your long-term ministry more efficient and productive.

● **Resources**—Smaller churches almost always need resources, and evaluation costs money. Assessment tools such as photocopied surveys add up, but the bigger cost usually comes in repairing the flaws flushed out by evaluation. Some improvements, such as necessary changes in curriculum, can have small price tags. Others may boast large price tags: salaries for additional staff members and the costs of building larger facilities.

While some small churches seek to correct smoldering problems before they burst into flame, many churches procrastinate until the only option is to let the fire burn itself out. A wiser course of action is to find the problems early and take care of them before they rage out of control.

There are low-cost/no-cost solutions for many problems. You'll find a discussion on this subject in Chapters 5 and 6. No matter what your ministry needs, there's a way to meet the needs, though finding the solutions may stretch your powers of creative problem-solving.

● **Fear of Failure and Fear of Change**—Too often smaller-church children's workers are afraid to change because they fear failure. Churches often avoid evaluation because they're afraid of the changes it will bring.

Even when proper evaluation takes place and changes are made, there's a chance that the changes won't work. Many small churches introduce change too quickly; without sufficient facilities, equipment, or finances; or without the necessary children or volunteer staff. Smaller churches can change more quickly than larger churches can, and they often plunge ahead before the structures are in place to make the change successful.

Smaller churches must allow time for big changes to take root. That includes giving the congregation time to get used to the change. If the congregation members can see the potential for positive results, they'll work through the change, even if it's uncomfortable at first.

Making Evaluation Work

Check out these principles for effective evaluation.

● **Keep it simple.** A well-designed half-page survey for each group will reap a better response than a five-page questionnaire.

● **Survey everyone.** Include children, parents, church leaders, the janitor, and anyone else involved with the church.

● **Evaluate your entire children's program regularly.** Evaluate curriculum, facilities, teachers, classroom experiences, specific programs (VBS, Sunday school, children's church), and children's attitudes. It's wiser to evaluate on a regular basis, little by little, than to undertake a huge annual assessment. If your program is evaluated after a rough quarter, it may make the whole year look worse than it was.

● **Keep your evaluations low-key.** If you're assessing a teacher, consider videotaping the class rather than watching from the corner. The teacher will be less nervous, and you will have a better glimpse into what the classroom is usually like.

● **Don't be secretive about the results.** Let people know what you discover, and they'll be better able to understand why you make changes.

● **Maintain the privacy of individuals.** If respondents are allowed to give their opinions anonymously, you'll probably get more accurate results. Few people in the church want to negatively evaluate each other. Maintain integrity at all costs.

● **Learn from others.** A simple evaluation of other churches in your area might help you to discover unmet needs that your church can address. Visit another children's program on a Sunday morning. Attend another church's vacation Bible school for a day. However, remember that in the final analysis it's not healthy to rate your ministry's effectiveness on the basis of what others are doing. Measure yourself against your own program objectives and goals.

● **When you can't survey everyone, survey a representative sample.** A successful survey will provide a snapshot of your ministry and will reveal potential dangers. To get accurate results, try to survey a cross section of respondents that truly represents your congregation.

● **Encourage participation.** Consider how many people will actually return their questionnaires. If one person in three participate, you'll have a good picture of attitudes, views, and ideas.

Proper evaluation takes work. But it's much better to conduct regular evaluations and to fix small problems than to plunge your head into the sand and ignore what's going wrong. Ignored problems never go away; they just get bigger.

Focusing Your Children's Ministry

These five basic steps will help you focus your ministry to children. Each step includes experiences that will get your volunteers talking. Consider using these steps in leadership training sessions.

Step One: Observe

Go to a place where children hang out, such as the churchyard, a park, or a fast-food restaurant. You could also walk through your neighborhood and observe the kids.

● What are they doing?
● What do they say to others?
● What do they see as fun?
● What do they play with?

Then consider your church's children.

- Are the interests similar? Why or why not?
- What activities do the children in our church and neighborhood most often engage in? Which ones could we, as a church, use as a doorway to ministry?
- Are there any unique needs in our situation? What are the financial, emotional, and community stresses in our area? How do church issues such as space, finances, and volunteer support affect our programs?
- In our situation, what's one thing we can do to reach the children in both our church and our surrounding neighborhood? How soon can we make it operational?

Step Two: Synthesize

Collect several old magazines and several photocopies of your church directory. If your church doesn't have a picture directory, write the name of each child in the church on a slip of paper.

Have your leadership volunteers tear out of the magazines pictures that represent the children in your church's neighborhood. Then tear pictures of children in your church from the photocopies of the directory. Group the neighborhood pictures and the church pictures separately. Ask:

- **What characteristics do these children share?**
- **What makes them different?**
- **What are their families like?**
- **What are the dynamics of our community and our neighborhood?**
- **How many churches with children's programs operate in our neighborhood?**
- **What needs are they not meeting that our congregation could meet?**

Step Three: Focus

Before the leadership training meeting, place a transparency with words (for example, a hymn, a praise chorus, or Scripture) on an overhead projector and manually make it severely out of focus. Turn it off. When you're ready for this activity, turn on the overhead projector and ask the volunteers to read what's on the transparency. Slowly focus the overhead projector until the words are clear. Ask:

• What can we learn from this experience about the importance of focusing our ministry to children?

• What programs does our church currently offer for children? Include seasonal events as well as all regular meetings.

• Read Matthew 28:19-20. What should be our primary objective in children's ministry?

• Now read 2 Timothy 3:14-17 and 1 John 4:9. What further objectives do these passages suggest?

As a group, review the list of programs your church presently offers to children. Place E's by those that primarily evangelize, D's by those that primarily disciple believers, EQ's by those that equip children to lead in the church, and L's by those that assure kids of God's love. Then ask:

• Which programs/events are our strengths? What areas are we weak in? Are the weak programs beyond help? Why or why not? What can we do to further strengthen our effective programs/events?

• What creative ideas/suggestions can our church develop to better evangelize children, to better mature them in the faith, and to better equip them for ministry?

Review the financial commitment your church can make to the children. Look at your volunteer base. Ask:

• Do we have the money and the people to run every program? Why or why not?

• Are there indispensable programs that we simply don't have funding for? What options are available? fund-raising opportunities?

Step Four: Adjust

Gather your volunteers in a room that can be almost

totally darkened. Turn off the lights, then ask people what they can see. Chat together as you allow several minutes to pass, then ask again what people can see. Most will see much better. Turn on the lights and watch the reactions. Ask:

- What was your first reaction to the darkness? to the light?
- How long did it take you to adjust?
- What does this experience say about adjusting our ministry to our changing situations?
- How is your ministry changing? Are there more or fewer children than there were last year? What predictions can you make about the changing needs of your children?
- How can you adjust your children's ministry programs in the anticipation of the changes that may come this year?

Step Five: Commit

Don't stop when you've come up with ideas. Commit yourselves to making any changes necessary to increase the effectiveness of your children's ministry.

Close your meeting with prayer. Ask for God's presence in your ministry. Ask also for God's leading and for discernment in making decisions that will guide your church's children toward growth in Christ.

CURRICULUM EVALUATION

Use these questions to analyze the strengths and weaknesses of your present curriculum.

1. What seems to be the overall goal of this material?
- ❏ teach historical facts
- ❏ teach Bible vocabulary
- ❏ emphasize understanding of relevant life principles
- ❏ clearly apply Scripture to students' daily lives

2. What are the implied objectives?
- ❏ teach
- ❏ cover a lot of material
- ❏ keep students busy
- ❏ maintain a quiet, orderly classroom
- ❏ impart learning
- ❏ give kids thorough understanding and retention
- ❏ help students think
- ❏ keep students active and learning

3. Which is most encouraged: lower- or higher-order thinking?
- ❏ fill-in-the-blank exercises
- ❏ word games/puzzles
- ❏ rote memorizations
- ❏ closed-ended fact questions
- ❏ discovery learning
- ❏ thought-provoking activities
- ❏ conceptual understanding
- ❏ open-ended thinking questions

4. How is the Bible approached?
- ❏ memorizing quotations
- ❏ telling stories from history
- ❏ packing as much as possible into each lesson
- ❏ emphasizing biblical details
- ❏ helping kids understand practical truths
- ❏ giving students guidance for their daily lives
- ❏ thoroughly examining and applying one Bible truth per lesson
- ❏ emphasizing essential teachings

5. Is the methodology more passive or active?
- ❏ methodology is passive
- ❏ teacher relays information
- ❏ students sit still
- ❏ one or two senses are involved
- ❏ teachers lecture
- ❏ students are the audience
- ❏ lessons are boring and tedious
- ❏ teachers tell
- ❏ methodology is active
- ❏ students discover truth
- ❏ students move around
- ❏ several senses are involved
- ❏ students discuss
- ❏ students learn by doing
- ❏ lessons are fun and captivating
- ❏ teachers ask

6. What are the structures of learning?
- ❏ learning is individual or competitive
- ❏ students rely on teachers
- ❏ teachers do all the teaching
- ❏ curriculum is teacher-based
- ❏ learning is interactive: students work in pairs or small groups
- ❏ students rely on each other
- ❏ students often learn from each other
- ❏ curriculum is student-based

RATING THE CURRICULUM

Responses on the left side of this form indicate less effective learning approaches. Responses on the right side indicate approaches that result in more genuine learning.

TEACHING EVALUATION

Teacher: _____

Date: _____

How to grade: Observe a class personally or by video and rate each area with a number between one and 10, with 10 indicating excellence.

_____ **1. adventure (Were the students excited and challenged?)**

_____ **2. fun and captivation (Was the material enjoyable to learn?)**

_____ **3. involvement (Was everyone involved in the lesson?)**

_____ **4. student-based environment (Were the learners allowed to come to the conclusions?)**

_____ **5. discovery (Did the learners discover any new truths?)**

_____ **6. debriefing (Was there adequate exploration of the activities?)**

_____ **7. interaction (Were students involved in relating to one another?)**

_____ **8. appearance (Was the teacher properly dressed and groomed?)**

_____ **9. preparation (Was the teacher well prepared?)**

_____ **10. lesson results (Were the objectives met? Did the children apply the Bible to their lives?)**

SUGGESTIONS FOR IMPROVEMENT

CLASSROOM EVALUATION

Name or number of classroom: _____

For ages:_____

Room size: _____ feet by _____ feet   Total square feet:_____

Room Size

Preschoolers (0 to 5 years) need 30 to 35 square feet per child. Older children (6 to 12 years) need 25 to 30 square feet per child. Use these guidelines to determine the appropriateness of your room sizes.

Total square feet of room_____ ÷ _____ (30 for preschoolers or 25 for older children) = _____ total number of children this room accommodates.

Current attendance _____ × _____ (30 for preschoolers or 25 for older children) = _____ total square feet needed for current number of children.

This classroom size is (circle one)
• larger than necessary for present class size,
• appropriate for present class size, or
• too small for present class size.

Other Factors

Using the following questions, rate each classroom with a number between one and 10, with 10 indicating excellence.

____Is the classroom clean, neat, and free of clutter?

____Does the room feature colorful posters, appealing paint, and clean window coverings and carpets?

____Is the classroom free (or protected) from potential hazards for the children who use it (sharp corners, electrical outlets, items that could be swallowed)?

____Is there appropriate storage for curriculum materials and supplies (out of reach of younger students)?

____Does the room invite learning about the Bible (pleasant to enter and appealing to eye, nose, and touch)?

____Is the classroom properly stocked with learning supplies appropriate to the age group?

____Is there quick access to water fountains and bathrooms?

____Are there appropriate furnishings for the age group (tables, chairs, coat racks)?

Chapter Three

SMALL SUCCESSES

"Don't look at how handsome Eliab is or how tall he is... God does not see the same way people see. People look at the outside of a person, but the Lord looks at the heart"

(1 Samuel 16:7).

The small businesses in Hudson, New York, had a big problem that small churches can learn from.

A Wal-Mart store came to the neighboring city of Greenport. When Wal-Mart comes to town, many small businesses close their doors. Why? Because Wal-Mart is a huge chain of big stores that are clean and sell things for low prices.

Keepers of smaller shops simply can't compete with the prices at Wal-Mart. As Wal-Mart has marched across America, thousands of smaller businesses have lost customers, sales, and profits. Many small businesses must reduce staff and accept meager profits just to remain open.

The small businesses in Hudson knew they couldn't beat Wal-Mart, but they didn't want to give up. So they decided to look for opportunities instead of focus on the obstacles. They inventoried their stores, gathered data, and created a master plan.

The first part of their plan was that each store be unique. Hudson shopkeepers developed inventories that focused on specific items. While Wal-Mart had two aisles for greeting cards and three more for toys, the small businesses created whole stores for such items. They didn't carry the same inventory that Wal-Mart and other local stores stocked. Instead they offered completely *new* and *unique* cards, toys, and other items.

Personal service was the second part of the plan. Wal-Mart would employ a larger staff and offer consumers more options than the smaller stores would. Yet the size of the store would also limit unique personal services that are attractive to shoppers. So the smaller stores decided to concentrate on providing home deliveries, quick special orders, and personal charge accounts. And they made it a point to know each customer by name.

The final part of the plan may have been the most important. The Hudson shopkeepers knew they needed to stay positive. They believed in themselves and their dreams. Even though they faced a mighty corporate giant, they also recognized their own ability to provide service.

"In Sunday school we learned how Jesus made a thousand meals from some bread and fish. My mom can do the same thing with Thanksgiving leftovers!"

As a smaller church, you often face formidable foes much stronger and bigger than you are. Once you recognize them, you can neutralize these monsters through creativity and sweat. Be aware of the foes you face.

● The Volunteer Viper—Most small churches suffer from a volunteer shortage, but we often overlook potential volunteers. Children's ministry volunteers can be parents, senior citizens, singles, and even teenagers. Chapter 5 will specifically address this obstacle.

● The Money Monster—Small churches naturally have tight budgets. In children's ministry, that means walking away from some good (and costly) programming. The answer is in being creative. Seek out resources available in your church and community. Chapter 6 will discuss this issue more fully.

● Count Numeral—Have you ever planned the greatest event that nobody came to? Remember the frustration? Low turnout occurs in every program, no matter how big or small the church. Be careful how you react to low attendance. Don't concern yourself with who's *not* there; instead celebrate those who do attend your activity, even if only one child shows up.

● The Space Alien—Lack of space can be a huge obstacle in children's programming, especially within the small church. Small churches often put children in "leftover" space such as hallways, storage rooms, and attics. But even such less-than-ideal places can be adapted for success. One secret is to let the kids "own" their space, no matter where it is. The kids will enjoy meeting anywhere as long as the area is theirs.

● The Envy Ghoul—It's difficult to feel content in smaller-church ministry. It's easy to be envious of the facilities and budgets of larger churches. But numbers are relative, and so is success. It's far better to succeed in a few areas than to fail—or settle for mediocrity—in many.[1]

They didn't need 20 checkout stands or 30 aisles or 200 employees to be successful. And they refused to allow obstacles to hide their opportunities.

Your smaller-church children's ministry can learn from the Hudson shopkeepers. Develop the traits that make your church unique. Inventory your children's ministry menu to see what's attracting children and meeting their needs. In your church it might be vacation Bible school, backyard Bible clubs, a special recreation time on Saturday afternoons, or your children's choir. Pour your energy into what works, giving it every opportunity to grow and reach its potential.

Personal service is also a smaller-church advantage. The small church can change in an instant to meet the special needs of individuals. And the small church can provide a close, loving, family atmosphere that just can't exist in a church with 1,000 members.

Most important, stay positive! Don't get bogged down in the "if onlys" that plague smaller-church ministries: "If only we had a budget for a brand-new curriculum every year," "If only we had at least 15 children," or "If only we had a trained volunteer for each age level." Instead of wishing for more, take what you've got and make it special.

Leading a smaller-church ministry within a few miles of larger churches can be disheartening. It's hard to witness their dynamic programs and not feel like a failure.

Either we can be disappointed by comparing ourselves to others or we can make the most of our own strengths and opportunities. Every church is different, and small churches, like small businesses, must sometimes create their own opportunities.

Becoming a David

The story of David, the shepherd boy, has always intrigued me. I've often wondered what his mother thought as he sat down for supper and told about knocking off lions and bears, how his dad felt when Samuel anointed David king of Israel, or what his older brothers whispered when he refused to wear Saul's armor and walked out alone—with a sling and a few stones—to face Goliath.

David wasn't concerned about what other people

thought or what he couldn't do. Instead he concentrated on what God could do through him. His young age and small stature didn't matter.

The smaller church can learn a lesson from this shepherd boy. Too often we worry about what we *can't* do rather than seek what God can do through us. We unnecessarily weigh ourselves down as we attempt to don a larger church's "armor" in program, facility, or mission. Instead we must let our smaller-church children's ministry be itself, casting aside kingly armor and picking up pebbles.

The question now becomes *How?*

Go, Go, Go

I believe that "go" is the most important part of the gospel. Go into all the world. Go to the neighborhoods. Go to the malls. Go where the children live.

Unfortunately, the plan of many small churches is to wait until people come. Small churches send out the word: "Come to our Sunday school. Come to our event. Come to our building." But children (and their parents) don't come.

Effective churches learn to enter their world through programs and people, to meet the unchurched on their turf. George Barna, in *User Friendly Churches,* comments that such churches attract people who feel that Christianity isn't just about being ministered to. Rather, these people want to be challenged to use their gifts and resources to serve others.[2]

In my national study of smaller-church children's ministries, very few churches had developed strategies for reaching into their neighborhoods. Most were content to produce children's programs at church, such as VBS, Awana, and Royal Rangers, hoping to attract outsiders. While such programs may attract new *Christian* families, they rarely will catch the eye of the unchurched.

Growing churches have learned that growing means going. Again, the smaller church can claim an advantage. A small church's neighbors may not always attend the church, but they usually accept and support its existence. Neighbors rarely see small churches—whether urban or rural—as threatening. Around larger churches, neighbors are often distrustful of the church. Some larger churches must constantly smooth ruffled neighborhood feathers. Because a small church already possesses a positive image in the neighborhood, it's easier for a small church to have an impact on surrounding families.

Any smaller church can design a children's ministry that reaches out to kids—a program geared to "go." Backyard vacation Bible schools easily attract unchurched children. So do Bible clubs and just-for-fun activities at people's homes. Even Sunday school can occasionally be moved outside the church walls. A children's ministry on the *go* will reap a harvest of children who will *come*.

Use Active Learning

We adults tend to teach the way we've been taught. We often concentrate on pouring biblical facts into the brains of our students. Unfortunately, lectures and discussions are weak teaching methods for children. Head knowledge doesn't necessarily produce heart faith or even inspire behavioral change.

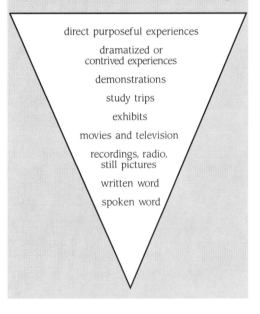

How We Learn

Children retain more when they're involved in the learning experience. The top of this cone depicts learning methods that utilize the learner's own experience. The bottom shows learning methods that rely on the experience of others. The learning methods are ranked from top to bottom, with the most effective methods at the top.[3]

direct purposeful experiences

dramatized or contrived experiences

demonstrations

study trips

exhibits

movies and television

recordings, radio, still pictures

written word

spoken word

Children welcome activity, and they learn best by doing. Smaller churches overflow with opportunities for hands-on experiences that help children learn about God.

In *Why Nobody Learns Much of Anything at Church: And How to Fix It*, Thom and Joani Schultz give a compelling analysis of contemporary Christian education. In this book, the authors list several "misguided barometers" that churches employ to test their educational efforts, including

- "Our classrooms are well-disciplined and quiet,"
- "We're using this theologically correct material,"
- "Our teachers have no complaints with the material we're using," and
- "The children are busy the whole hour."[4]

As the Schultzes correctly point out, none of these barometers measures the *goal* of Christian education. Our purpose in teaching children is not to have well-disciplined classes, smiling teachers, or busy children. The goal of Christian education is *changed lives.*

That's the appeal of active learning.

Active learning involves action and kids' senses to teach truth. The pungent odors of a zoo can communicate volumes about "arkeology" and Noah. A teaspoon of salt mixed with sugar can teach bittersweet lessons about blending faith with worldliness. Helping to clean up an elderly person's yard can provide learning about servanthood that will last a lifetime.

Our faith is a living faith. It cannot be developed through academic exercises alone. And children are concrete thinkers. Because of their natural cognitive stage, kids must have lessons "with handles." They must be able to grasp and experience a truth before they can own it. Active learning gives them those handles.

The smaller church is the perfect arena for active learning experiences. A small class naturally welcomes the flexibility and "teachable moments" that make active learning incredibly effective. Discussions reach deeper insights with only a few students. And teacher-student relationships developed through active learning can be even more meaningful when classes are small.

Resource Spotlight:

Why Nobody Learns Much of Anything at Church: And How to Fix It

Every now and then a book comes along and sets a new standard. *Why Nobody Learns Much of Anything at Church: And How to Fix It,* by Thom and Joani Schultz, is one of those books (Group Publishing, 1993).

In this book, the Schultzes not only give an insightful evaluation of learning in the church, but also offer scores of creative, practical, active learning ideas. It's a must-read for every small-church teacher, Sunday school superintendent, church leader, and minister.

It's important to use theologically correct curriculum and to provide materials the teachers like. However, the goal of Christian education must be to help kids learn and apply biblical truth—to help them know, love, and follow Jesus. Active learning will help you reach that goal.

Emphasize the Family

Perhaps the greatest advantage in working within a smaller church is that children's ministry can be true *family* ministry. The larger a church grows, the more it tends to separate people into age groups. Each additional staff person specializes and further separates his or her ministry area from the rest of the congregation: children's ministries, youth ministries, singles ministries, senior adult ministries, music ministries, and the list goes on.

Interestingly enough, a recent trend in larger churches has been the hiring of family ministers to encourage and minister to families in the church. But for now, the divisions still exist. In contrast, the smaller church *already* promotes family ministry. The smaller the church, the greater the edge in family ministry. A church of 50 members can more easily produce a solid family ministry than a church of 150 because its members interact with each other more.

Family Fun

Have fun promoting closeness in families with these great activities. You'll find that neighborhood families are attracted to the positive benefits of this kind of ministry:

- a family kickball game (parents vs. kids, church leaders vs. everyone else, families whose last names begin with the letters from A through L against those whose names begin with the letters from M through Z);
- a family potluck picnic in the park;
- a family Bible study in a neighborhood home;
- family-worship Sundays (base the service around families worshiping together);
- family portraits (take photos of families and post them in a prominent place or make a church directory);
- family YMCA or gymnasium nights (public schools often rent out gyms for little cost);
- family activities such as bowling, roller-skating, and miniature golfing; and
- family trips to zoos, ballparks, theaters, or local places of interest.

Try these ideas that a smaller-church children's ministry can pull off.

● **Mobile Sunday school**—If you have a church van or can borrow one, hold your Sunday school lessons in it on occasion. Travel to area parks or homes for special lesson activities. Use the van for discussion times. Tour the neighborhood and stop at a street corner (where children are playing) to present a brief object lesson. The sky's the limit!

● **Movie madness**—Show videos on Friday nights. Hold monthly living room video showings, featuring Disney, comedy, and family features. To avoid copyright infringement, check with the company holding the copyright on any movie you plan to show.

● **Living life-of-Christ tour**—Take your children on a whirlwind tour of Christ's life, using "on location" activities. Travel to a barn and talk about Jesus' birth. Go to a stream and talk about his baptism. At a tall building, discuss his temptation by Satan. Go to a hill or a knoll to talk about the Sermon on the Mount. A flower garden is a good setting for a talk on the Garden of Gethsemane. At a cemetery, discuss his death and resurrection. This tour can be done in half a day or over several weeks. Travel logistics make this activity difficult with more than 10 kids.

● **Bicycle progressive dinner**—This is just like the traditional progressive dinner, except the children ride their bikes between courses. This works best with a group of four to eight children who live within several blocks of each other.

● **VBS on location**—Take your vacation Bible school "on location" this summer. Choose your location based on your theme: Animals (hold VBS at a local farm), Sun and Surf (go to the beach), Wild West (head for a ranch), Baseball (hold VBS on a ball diamond), or Camping With Christ (head for the woods).

Unfortunately, many small churches try to be like larger churches and create programs that separate age groups.

One Pennsylvania church of 60 people began a Wednesday-night kids' program. If 10 kids—between ages 2 and 16—showed up, it was a good night. While the adults had a Bible study, the kids had their own meeting. But rarely were there enough kids to even play a game. And the leaders struggled to provide activities that would interest and fit all the kids. What a frustrating situation! Since the Sunday programming already divided the church into age-specific groups, the church could have better used Wednesday nights to create a family-ministry evening. They could have included creative opportunities for families to grow closer to God together.

Another small church, in the St. Louis area, has created an exciting family ministry that also reaches out to the community. They've expanded a formerly traditional VBS program into a Family Festival. The program—geared to reach the whole family—features adult seminars on special issues and creative activities designed to attract unchurched kids.

Be Different

The small church is different.

Church-growth specialist Lyle Schaller made that point over a decade ago, and he's still on target. The smaller congregation is unique, with natural strengths and gifts that larger churches wish they had.

Unfortunately, the smaller church tends to assume that what works with 1,000 people can be pared down to work with 100. George Barna countered this assumption when he said, "In the context of church growth, imitation is…the quickest route to doom. Ministry by mimicry almost invariably results in deterioration, rather than growth."[5]

It's easy to see how the small church gets caught up in ministry by mimicry. How many of these statements sound familiar?

"Everybody else has a vacation Bible school…"

"We need to hire a children's minister—that's what First Church did."

"There's this dynamic church in [some large city], and they…"

"What we really need is a gymnasium."

Such attitudes can cripple a smaller congregation. When they attempt to imitate larger churches—whether in programming, staffing, facilities, resources, or curriculum—they actually limit their own freedom and opportunities. Many small churches, especially those who pursue a bigger-is-better-at-any-cost philosophy, extend themselves beyond their gifts, abilities, and resources.

Instead, smaller churches should celebrate their uniqueness and individuality. Dare to be different. Be a David. Don't worry about your size and appearance, but focus on what God can do through you. Seek to reach children around you and bring them to maturity in Jesus Christ. Rejoice in what you do well! Dream big, but don't live beyond your size. A church of 60 people should be a dynamic church of 60, not a church that yearns to be a church of 600.

Catch a vision of what your church can do right now, and let God guide you into the future.

Creating Vision

A smaller-church children's ministry must envision what it can accomplish through God's power. I call this "Red Sea thinking." When the Israelites were caught between a wide sea and an unbeatable Egyptian army, Moses relied on Red Sea thinking. Initially, not everyone believed. But when the water rolled back and created an opportunity for escape, no one remained behind. A person with Red Sea thinking puts faith in God, not man. Red Sea thinking doesn't allow obstacles to negate opportunities. People with Red Sea thinking do what they can with the resources available, then allow God to work miracles. And even the skeptics will follow.

Vision is crucial to effective ministry. It allows you to look ahead and purposefully plan today for a specific outcome tomorrow. But visionary thinking isn't always easy.

George Barna, in *The Power of Vision*, describes deadly traps that can ambush visionaries within the church, five of which are tradition, fear, complacency, fatigue, and short-term thinking.[6] These five snares pose particular danger in smaller churches. Tradition can trap leaders

("We've *always* done it that way!"), and so can fear ("How will we afford this program if any more families leave the church?"). Complacency ("I really don't care; my kids are already grown") and fatigue ("I give up! I've been at this for six years and nothing ever changes!") present similar dangers. And short-term thinking ("We need to take care of these kids now. We don't have time to worry about next year!") can quickly snuff out effective ministry.

Thankfully, David didn't allow tradition ("You're just a shepherd boy!"), fear ("He's going to smash you, kid!"), complacency ("Someone else can fight the giant."), fatigue ("I've traveled a long way just to get here."), or even short-term thinking ("I'll wait until I'm older.") to deter him from clobbering Goliath. David had a solid vision that looked past the traps and obstacles, seeing what God could do.

Part of developing a vision for children's ministry is considering what kinds of programming might meet the various needs of the children in your church and your community. And that leads us right into the next chapter.

....

1. Rick Chromey, "Big Thinking in a Small Church," CHILDREN'S MINISTRY Magazine (March/April 1993), 13-14.

2. George Barna, *User Friendly Churches* (Ventura, CA: Regal Books, 1991), 34.

3. Edgar Dale, *Audiovisual Methods in Teaching* (Holt, Rinehart and Winston, Inc., 1969).

4. Thom and Joani Schultz, *Why Nobody Learns Much of Anything at Church: And How to Fix It* (Loveland, CO: Group Publishing, Inc., 1993), 14-15.

5. Barna, *User Friendly Churches,* 16.

6. George Barna, *The Power of Vision* (Ventura, CA: Regal Books, 1992), 122-129.

Chapter Four

BALANCED MINISTRY

"Anyone who lives on milk is still a baby and knows nothing about right teaching. But solid food is for those who are grown up. They have practiced in order to know the difference between good and evil"

(Hebrews 5:13-14).

In many ways, planning programs for a smaller-church children's ministry is like planning nutritious meals. Small children don't eat a lot, so their food must be packed with nutrition. Small children can be finicky, too, so food must look good and taste great. In a small church, resources are limited, so every program must bring a return in spiritual growth and commitment that justifies the output of time, energy, and money. Also, small churches must provide exciting programs that attract people.

We know about children's nutritional needs. But children have spiritual needs, too. They need to be exposed to Christian fellowship, Bible study, and service opportunities to grow into strong, healthy Christians.

We also need to realize that children's needs are different from adults' needs. Children think differently. They respond to situations differently. And they involve themselves with others differently. Children are active, and they delight in games and noise. Our programs must meet children at different levels cognitively, physically, and spiritually. Children must not be viewed as underdeveloped, as inferior, or even as mini-adults.

Our expectations for children's behavior may need some adjustment. It's unreasonable to expect 5-year-old Bobby to spend an hour in worship without a squirm or a fidget, a whisper or a question. It's next to impossible for him. An adult may think that if children are sitting still, they are listening. But the children may be using all of their mental energy to make themselves sit still and as a result may not be hearing anything. To be able to listen, children need freedom to move.

An effective children's minister will consider child development in preparing a well-balanced buffet of activities that deepen children's faith in God. Planning that buffet may challenge a smaller church because the buffet will be

smaller than it could be in a large church. Small churches have to pack everything children need into a smaller assortment of activities.

A Balanced Buffet

Every children's ministry should consist of four main areas of programming. The key to strong spiritual growth in children is a balance of these four areas similar to the balance of nutrition in meals:

● appetizers (non-threatening activities that reach out to all children),

● breads (opportunities for children to use their talents and interests in a low-level commitment to the church),

● vegetables (Bible studies that help children learn the basics of faith), and

● meats (service opportunities that help children mature and develop leadership skills).

Appetizers

Every smaller-church children's ministry should include non-threatening, just-for-fun activities to which children can bring unchurched friends. These "appetizer" activities are important to your ministry because they make children want more. They also give you a chance to really get to know the kids your ministry serves.

Adults are often tempted to sneak meat into the appetizer time. Some leaders are convinced that every church activity *must* have a biblical focus. So they go roller-skating and surprise the kids with a 25-minute Bible lesson afterward.

Small churches lean toward such thinking because they want to be thrifty in their use of volunteers and other resources. And, because *unchurched* kids are there, it's natural for people to want to toss in a little Bible study. But be wary of giving in to that temptation, because it may ruin kids' appetites. Children feel tricked when adults advertise fun and games and then force-feed them a Bible study. Program some activities that are just for fun, then watch for kids whose mouths water for something more.

Fun times also let you observe children and discover

Smaller churches often overlook the task of developing a philosophy for programming. Here are a few pointers to help you make sure your buffet is well thought out.

- **People come first.**

Successful restaurants live by this creed. The smaller-church children's ministry must be careful not to forget the children. Emphasize people, not programs. Too many small churches allow tradition to govern children's programming. Our children's ministries are the most effective when we keep our focus on meeting the needs of children.

- **If it doesn't work, try something else.**

Too many small churches serve up unattractive and unhealthy programs that don't satisfy the needs of today's children. Programs that prompt children to leave the table foster apathy and waste valuable resources (time, money, and volunteers). Even if children loved a program five years ago, kids won't necessarily find it appetizing today.

- **Make it affordable.**

It does little good to offer caviar to families who can only afford tuna. Don't plan too many costly activities, especially if some families have several children in your program. Five dollars doesn't sound like much except to families who have to pay for three kids.

their needs. Unlike adults, children often don't recognize when they feel a need for a more fulfilling prayer life or a deeper understanding of serving others. Observing kids during fun activities can help you plan your "menu" because you'll see where your children need to grow.

Breads

Appetizers will attract kids, but the bite-sized content of appetizers won't satisfy children's spiritual needs. The second level, "breads," aims at meeting children's basic spiritual needs such as fellowship and the knowledge that God

Krazy Kickball

Here's a fun, cooperative twist to the game of Kickball that can be played with as few as six participants. The rules are few: one pitch and one kick, with no foul balls (everything's fair). Catching a kicked ball in the air is the only way to make an out. The side is retired when all its players have kicked once or when three outs are recorded.

Now for the fun part: When the ball is kicked, the entire kicking team must form a tight group and the kicker must run around the group. If the ball isn't caught in the air, every trip around the group scores a run. The entire kicking team helps count.

If the ball isn't caught in the air, the fielding team must retrieve it and throw it to the pitcher. At the same time, the entire fielding team must line up, standing one behind the other, legs apart, behind the pitcher. Once the line is formed, the pitcher must pass the ball between his or her legs to the next person in line, who then passes it on between his or her legs. The ball must pass through the legs of the entire team. When the ball reaches the end, it must be passed back to the pitcher. When the pitcher receives the ball again, he or she yells "stop." The score is the number of times the kicker ran all the way around his or her team. The fielding team scatters around the field again and another child kicks.

Play at least three innings and be prepared for scores into the hundreds!

loves them. Like appetizers, bread activities are nonthreatening. But unlike appetizers, they begin to strengthen faith and meet inner needs with real answers. These activities show children that faith is a part of everyday life.

Just about any weekly children's meeting, other than Sunday school, qualifies as a "bread" program. Ministry groups such as children's choirs, puppet groups, and drama troupes are excellent programs. They're fun and they allow children to explore their faith.

If you have a few children of various ages, the children can play games or watch movies with spiritual messages. You can develop a club around children's interests such as coin collecting, flowers, or model rockets. You can also find out what concerns your children and discuss topics that interest them. Explore how faith in God relates to the topic and close with a brief prayer time. If your school district allows it, you can eat lunch with the children once a week and talk about a different subject each time. Or you can meet at an ice cream parlor after school or meet at church on a Saturday morning for a simple breakfast.

Group-building activities also belong in this level of programming. Cliques are common in small churches, and such activities can encourage a "whole group" mentality. For example, hold human-pyramid races with no more than three per team, then discuss teamwork. Or play a game of Krazy Kickball (see instructions on page 49) and talk about the difference between cooperation and competition.

Bread activities give children a chance to develop friendships and talents as they learn to apply their faith to everything they do. But children need special time to learn the basics of faith. That's where the next programming level comes in.

Vegetables

In most cases, "vegetables" are the backbone of a children's ministry, seeking to lead children to a deeper faith in God. Programs such as Sunday school, vacation Bible school, and children's church are vegetables. They do even more than teach children about the Christian faith; they moti-

It's possible to feed too much good programming to children. Over-programming cripples your program by tiring volunteers and saturating kids with activities. After a while, leaders and children alike will lose their enthusiasm. But how do you know when enough's enough?

Every church's program-saturation point is different. Sometimes that point is dictated by the financial base of the families in your church. Kids in low-income areas can't afford many activities that require them to bring money. The time of year can affect how much programming you can successfully carry out. For example, in rural areas, it's wise to program lightly during planting and harvesting times. Here are some hints for developing your programming buffet.

● Start by planning only one "extra" monthly program at each level. For example, you may plan one fun activity (appetizer), regular Wednesday night meetings (bread), and Sunday school (vegetable). Then, if you see a few kids have service or leadership potential, involve them in "meaty" service projects within the church body.

● Add new programs and events only as interest demands. Survey the children. Talk to their parents. If few will sign on to sing in a kids' choir, find a better use of your time.

● Learn from parental feedback about activities that require too much time or cost and about the number of activities you plan. Remember that families with several children will be the first ones to feel the squeeze of over-programming.

● Get your kids' school calendars and plan around important school events. If you're in a multi-school congregation, you may have difficulty doing this, but do your best to coordinate activities.

● Consider combining age-level activities into family nights. For example, instead of taking the juniors bowling one day and the middlers another, plan a family bowling night and encourage families to spend time with each other. Parents will like the idea. Kids will, too.

● Simply take a look at your schedule. If you're having trouble getting to all of the functions you've planned, the children are probably having trouble too.

vate children to find their roles within the church. Many small churches serve this course very well.

The smaller church has an advantage when it comes to vegetable programming because it can personalize its programming more easily than a larger church can. Children have more opportunities to ask questions, and leaders have far more flexibility in answering them. Teachers in small classes can tailor their curricula to the needs of the children who attend. One small church actually held a sixth-grade girls class with only one member! That child received an incredible education from a devoted mentor and friend.

Children need a heaping helping of the vegetable prayer. At this level, children are ready to participate in "share and prayer" opportunities. Again, small is best when it comes to prayer. By praying in groups of three or four, children will form close relationships. And they'll be able to see more clearly how their prayers are answered because every child will have a chance to participate—no one gets lost in the shuffle. You might encourage children to write or draw prayer requests on the church parking lot with colorful sidewalk chalk. Or have a "prayer scavenger hunt": Children seek out objects that best represent prayer needs in their lives.

Vegetable programming is your opportunity to teach children the basics of faith: what happened in the Bible and how we can respond to it. If presented creatively and experientially, these lessons will help children build a foundation for a lifetime.

Meat

This element of a children's programming buffet helps children use their abilities and gifts to serve God. "Meat" programming is the most difficult for children because it begins to grow them into leaders. It requires responsibility, dedication, and perseverance. But when we challenge and encourage children to use their gifts in important opportunities, we help them grow toward even more significant roles as they get older.

In my research on small-church children's ministries, I found very few churches that have developed this level of programming. Reaching this level is difficult. Small churches, however, have an advantage because they are usually more open to letting children serve.

Meat activities encourage children to reach out into their neighborhood, their school, their church, and their community through their own gifts and abilities. Children at this level rarely need a lot of encouragement. Once they catch the vision of what they can do for God, it'll be hard to stop them.

Meat programming doesn't have to be complicated. Children learn from small projects as well as large projects. Sometimes meat activities involve children in small tasks such as washing dishes, sweeping the fellowship hall, or carrying out trash. Again, the smaller church has an advantage because in a small church there are always more jobs than people. You might involve your sixth-graders in big projects such as leading backyard Bible studies for younger children. Through big and small activities, children learn that even they can contribute to God's work.

In most settings, the older children will be best prepared for meat programs, though younger children can be involved in limited ways. Preschoolers are too young for most service projects, but they can make no-bake cookies for the pastor or share hugs with senior church members. Middle-graders are ready participants because they are eager to please others. And sixth graders can even lead some of these activities with adult supervision.

A balanced smaller-church children's program will feature service-oriented opportunities for children. And while such programs may not be easy to prepare or lead, they'll produce incredible growth in the lives of your children.

Small Helpings Work, Too

Some might say it's impossible in a small church to provide programming in all four of the areas we've just looked at. But with proper balancing, you'll find that it can be done. You don't need to provide all of these levels on an *ongoing* basis for every age group in your church. Vary your programming to suit your attendance and to get the most from your resources.

Let the children be your measuring stick. If the children in your church are growing and excited about God, then your ministry is successful even if your calendar doesn't show a children's activity for every type of opportunity. You may find that once you have several children involved in vegetable meetings, you'll be able to forget about appetizers for a few months.

Also, almost every idea in this chapter can be adapted, altered, or arranged in a manner suitable to even the smallest children's group. Naturally, some games (such as Krazy Kickball) require a minimum number of participants, but many do not.

Tailor your buffet to the needs of your kids. Add and subtract programs as the children in your church develop and grow. Provide a balanced program for your children—one that is creative, is well planned, and offers a smorgasbord of options for children at all stages of faith.

AWESOME APPETIZERS FOR LITTLE OR NO COST

These nonthreatening activities help unchurched kids feel welcome.

AGES 3 TO 6	AGES 6 TO 8	AGES 8 TO 12
1. parent/child nature walks	1. zoo trips	1. bike riding
2. play-at-the-park parties	2. visits to local farms	2. in-line skating
3. stuffed-animal pet shows	3. bike rides or races	3. nature hikes
4. Barney/Sesame Street parties	4. pumpkin-pickin' parties	4. art projects
5. parent/child artwork classes	5. games at the park	5. zoo trips
	6. picnics	6. natural-history museums
	7. formal tea parties (girls)	7. airports/aviation museums
	8. baseball-card parties (boys)	8. bowling
		9. neighborhood pet shows
		10. pool parties
		11. roller-skating

Guidelines

● Ages 3 to 6: Children of this age don't relate well with each other, but this is a great opportunity to reach parents. One activity every four to six months is about right.

● Ages 6 to 8: Exclusive boy or girl parties are always successful! Try to hold them on the same day at different locations. One activity per quarter is sufficient.

● Ages 8 to 12: Publicity with this age group is crucial. Children of this age group have more choices and demands on their time. Be sure to communicate to both child and parent. Always have plenty of adult supervision (at least one adult for every five children). One activity per quarter usually works well, with a few extra activities scheduled during the summer months.

SENSATIONAL BREADS FOR LITTLE OR NO COST

These low-level commitments will introduce children to the church and will build friendships.

AGES 3 TO 6	AGES 6 TO 8	AGES 8 TO 12
1. cherub choir	1. children's choir	1. children's dramas
2. weekly topical meetings	2. weekly topical meetings	2. weekly topical meetings
3. vacation Bible school (VBS)	3. vacation Bible school (VBS)	3. vacation Bible school (VBS)
4. seasonal parties	4. seasonal parties	4. seasonal parties
5. Bible-school open house	5. Bible-school open house	5. Bible-school open house
6. bring-a-friend balloon day	6. photo day: children photograph each other or the neighborhood	6. video game tournaments
	7. in-church pizza parties	7. puppet plays
	8. parents' nights out	8. lock-ins and overnighters

Guidelines

● Ages 3 to 6: Because of the need for heavy parental/adult involvement, two activities per year will be sufficient.

● Ages 6 to 8: Allow children to develop abilities without a lot of pressure. Affirm children often, especially for life skills such as willingness to follow directions, to obey teachers, and to share. Have parents serve as helpers (children of this age welcome their parents). One activity per quarter is sufficient.

● Ages 8 to 12: Allow children to plan some activities. Encourage kids to participate and bring friends. One activity every other month is plenty.

VALUABLE VEGGIES
FOR LITTLE OR NO COST

These weekly Bible studies will help children mature both individually and as a faith community.

AGES 3 TO 6	AGES 6 TO 8	AGES 8 TO 12
1. Sunday school	1. Sunday school	1. Sunday school
2. cherub church	2. children's worship	2. junior worship
3. vacation Bible school (VBS)	3. vacation Bible school (VBS)	3. vacation Bible school (VBS)
4. story times	4. backyard Bible studies	4. backyard Bible studies
5. parent/child Bible stories	5. Christian-movie parties	5. Christian-movie parties
		6. midweek Bible studies

Guidelines

● Ages 3 to 6: Repetition is vital! A structure with consistency will help these children learn best. Keep concepts simple.

● Ages 6 to 8: Repetition and consistency remain key. Emphasize Bible stories and life application.

● Ages 8 to 12: Variety is important. Kids in this age group enjoy surprises. Vary your programming whenever possible. Expand children's horizons with deeper life application.

MARVELOUS MEATS FOR LITTLE OR NO COST

With these ministry opportunities, children will serve others and develop leadership skills for future work in the church.

AGES 3 TO 6	AGES 6 TO 8	AGES 8 TO 12
1. draw pictures for senior saints	1. bake cookies for nursing home residents	1. help in the nursery
2. go Christmas caroling in nursing homes	2. make cards for shut-ins	2. lead children's worship
3. adopt grandparents	3. memorize Scripture and share verses in children's worship	3. help lead adult worship
4. sing special songs during worship services	4. help clean church building	4. read Scriptures
5. bring flowers to shut-ins	5. play or sing special music during worship	5. give devotions
	6. read easy Scriptures at children's worship	6. write songs
	7. organize a toy drive for homeless kids	7. create dramas
	8. collect presents for prisoners	8. play or sing special music during worship
	9. deliver flowers to sick people/shut-ins	9. create children's newsletter
		10. collect food for a food bank
		11. collect money for missions

Guidelines

• Ages 3 to 6: Create activities to match their short attention spans and memories. Outside activities should not last longer than one hour and should be kept to a minimum frequency.

• Ages 6 to 8: Children can now understand that their actions can make a difference, and they are open to helping others. One service project per quarter is perfect.

• Ages 8 to 12: Allow kids to choose their service emphasis. Provide praise and support as children share their lives with others. This age group can really get into service projects, but to keep interest (and commitment) high, schedule no more than one per month.

Chapter Five

FINDING HELP

"When he saw the crowds, he felt sorry for them because they were hurting and helpless, like sheep without a shepherd. Jesus said to his followers, 'There are many people to harvest but only a few workers to help harvest them'"

(Matthew 9:36-37).

The primary frustrations among smaller-church children's ministry coordinators are finding, training, and motivating volunteers. Finding the right volunteers can be tough. Those who are willing aren't always skilled. And it seems as if those who would really shine in ministry often say no. The phrase most frustrating to those in children's ministry may be "Get someone else."

We need to remember that it's not always easy to be a volunteer. Many people sincerely feel ill-equipped for leading children. This chapter will explore creative solutions to the problem of staffing children's programs in smaller churches.

Recruiting for Successful Ministry

Recruiting is a full-time job. It doesn't just happen in the month before the start of a new Sunday school year. Be on the lookout for volunteers at all times.

● **Look for volunteers of all occupations.** Volunteers aren't all alike. Some have been trained to teach, many have not. Some enjoy working personally with children, others welcome indirect children's ministry. A few can organize while others support. You may find an excellent volunteer who's a retired construction worker, a housewife who home-schools her children, a middle-aged single adult who's had little contact with kids, a father with five children, a janitor, or the CEO of a large company. Remember that age makes no difference. Some of the best children's workers are teenagers and older adults.

But should some people be avoided?

Les Christie, in his excellent book *Unsung Heroes,* suggests three types of volunteers to avoid.[1] First, avoid adults who want to recapture their childhood. Kids need an adult, not another kid, to lead them. Second, avoid adults who are content to merely chaperone. Volunteers are children's *workers.* They're not sponsors or even coaches. Children's ministry is hard work. Finally, Christie encourages the avoidance of adults who view their role as that of preachers. To work with children is to be more than a dispenser of moral advice. Sometimes children just need a hand to hold or a friend to play ball with. While our role is to teach children about Jesus, children should *see* Jesus in us as well.

● **Evaluate personal interests and gifts.** As you recruit, match people to positions. Organized adults can easily plan day trips, develop a curriculum, or design a children's program. Adults who enjoy writing can create a children's or parent's newsletter or can type up a recruitment letter. Drama enthusiasts can start a children's pup-

"I THINK WHAT MRS. NITWHIPPLE IS TRYING TO SAY IS THAT WE NEED HELP WITH THE SIXTH-GRADERS THIS MORNING."

pet ministry, provide dramas for children's worship, or develop a clown ministry. Musical adults can lead children's worship or choirs.

Sometimes you may need photographers, cooks, drivers, painters, publicists, seamstresses, typists, carpenters, fundraisers, missionaries, and teachers. Rather than recruit a few to wear many hats, recruit several people—with various gifts and interests—to wear a few hats each. It's easier to enlist someone for a 15-minute job than for a 15-hour tour of duty.

● **Recognize, reward, and restore your workers.** Successful recruitment incorporates affirmation of volunteers. Jot a note to every volunteer each month to express appreciation for each person's sacrifice and contribution in leading kids. Give workers time off. Keep a list of substitutes who will fill in every once in a while for a teacher who needs a week off.

Rewarding your volunteers can be great fun. January is a great month to designate as Children's Ministry Month. Create an annual celebration and spotlight your children's teachers, helpers, and workers. In a special worship service, present each worker with a flower or plaque. Host an appreciation dinner prepared and served by the children and parents. Feature workers in your church newsletter, weekly announcements, and bulletin boards.

Affirmation doesn't have to cost a lot of money. One small church in Colorado purchased a basket for each of its children's workers and invited the kids—during a morning worship service—to fill their teachers' baskets with fruit and to say thank you. The children of another small congregation serenaded their teachers with thank you songs set to the music of Christmas carols. To the tune of "Jingle Bells," they sang, "Thanks to you, thanks to you, for all the things you do."

Children's workers who quit generally do so because they feel used or tired. Affirming your teachers will restore their confidence and stamina and will improve their teaching. Also, public affirmations draw attention to your children's ministry and subsequently attract potential workers. Everyone wants to be on a winning team!

● **Create success early.** When we toss volunteers into situations beyond their ability, they'll likely become discouraged. And they'll probably say no when they're asked to renew their commitment.

On the other hand, volunteers who experience early success will enjoy their work and will be

When There's Nobody Left to Ask

It's not a pretty sight: You've got a class but no teacher. You've called everyone in the church directory and no one will help. What do you do? Here are a few possibilities.

● **Rotate parents.** Parents of the children in the class have the most at stake, so rotate them in to teach or help. This is less than ideal because children learn better when their classroom experience is stable.

● **Find someone who will team-teach with a teenager.** This is an especially good option for younger children. Make sure the adolescent is responsible and spiritually mature.

● **Rearrange the classes.** If you can't find a teacher for your third- and fourth-graders, try moving the third-graders in with the younger grades and the fourth-graders in with the older grades. This is often an acceptable solution unless your classes are already large.

● **Shut down the class.** It's a last-ditch option, but it's sometimes necessary. Notify the church at least three weeks ahead of time to make sure everyone gets word. Announcing the closing of a class will almost always produce a teacher, though he or she may be motivated by guilt. Give such a volunteer extra help and encouragement.

likely to stay. Start workers out on small, fun projects. Allow them to experience a small success such as going along on a trip to the zoo. Then begin to challenge them with larger jobs.

Schedule a training time for new teachers before they begin teaching. Then have new teachers team-teach for a few weeks with the outgoing teachers. Finally, have the new recruits teach the lessons under the observation of the outgoing teachers. With proper training, the new teacher is more likely to experience success early.

Choosing the Right Children's Workers

Having good volunteers is important. The wrong volunteer can alienate children or cause devastating damage to your program and reputation. A good volunteer must be faithful, available, and teachable.

● **Faithfulness**—A volunteer must be faithful to the church. Avoid any volunteer who hasn't been a regular part of the church for at least six months and who hasn't been a Christian for at least two years. Too often, newcomers are ushered into immediate service without a test of their faithfulness. A six-month waiting period will help you understand who they are and what they believe. Tragically, child molesters may come to churches to find children to abuse. A waiting period generally discourages people who are looking for quick access to children.

Volunteers must also be faithful to your program. They must welcome the opportunity to work within your organizational framework and philosophy of ministry. Children's ministry isn't a place for lone rangers. If volunteers don't want to work within your standards or sign your teaching contract, it's best to let them walk away, no matter how good they appear to be.

● **Availability**—A potential volunteer must be available to serve. Smaller-church adults tend to wear many hats. I've had to turn down some excellent workers because they were already too busy. Children's ministry requires time. Adults who are already over-committed to other responsibilities will be distracted volunteers, and their ministry will suffer. One standard I've attempted to uphold is that volunteers may commit to only one ministry within the

Team-teaching can help avoid potential problems. Many churches now employ the "two adult" rule. Two adults lead every class or activity where children are involved. This standard minimizes opportunities for misconduct by individuals, and it protects your volunteers from false accusations. The accountability also makes parents more comfortable.

Only a few small churches screen their volunteers who work with children. Few churches of any size require FBI background checks for potential children's volunteers. However, you might want to consider such screenings for children's workers. Child molesters often find easy access into churches, especially small churches that desperately need help and quickly move willing workers into leadership positions.

Drew Crislip, a West Virginia lawyer and children's camp director, suggests these ideas for screening potential volunteers:[2]

● **Use a detailed application form.** Get a written statement from the applicant that he or she has no background of impropriety with children.

● **Interview volunteers.** Develop a qualified team to interview potential workers. Local police or social service agencies can offer training or advice. Ask probing interview questions: Why are you interested in children's work? Have you ever been accused of impropriety?

● **Check for criminal activities.** Explain to applicants your purpose in using background checks. Get a written release from the applicant and complete a criminal records check. If an applicant refuses to cooperate, don't permit that person to work with children.

● **Contact references.** Request references from individuals who've known the applicant in many settings (personal, educational, and professional), even if the person is someone well known to your ministry.

● **Require a waiting period.** Wait at least six months before moving new applicants into ministry.

Many small churches will look at these suggestions and reply, "This all seems a bit unrealistic." Perhaps so. But unfortunately, those who fail to adequately screen their children's workers expose themselves to potential heartaches and lawsuits.

church. If someone is already teaching Sunday school, I don't recruit that person for a Wednesday-evening children's group.

- **Teachability**—Every volunteer must be willing to be trained. Regardless of academic degrees, age, and experience, everyone can learn something new. Schedule formal training once or twice a year. Make it fun and encourage the development of friendships among teachers. Consider having teachers meet once a week or once a month for a short time before or after church. This short meeting allows teachers to discuss how to teach individual lessons and how to provide for the needs of individual children.

Addressing Objections

A children's ministry coordinator can get discouraged by the explanations people give for not volunteering. Here are five of these reasons and ways you can address them.

"I'd rather work with teenagers or adults."

I recently spoke with a young man who'd just graduated from a Bible college. I hoped he'd work with our children's worship. After I outlined the children's worker position, he explained that such a ministry was beneath his ability, education, and calling. His response was disappointing. Unfortunately, many potential workers share his attitude.

To some, working with children is a waste of talent. Or it lacks glamour. After all, elementary-age craft projects and Bible school don't seem as exciting as the youth missions trip to Mexico.

So how do you motivate those who possess the ability and the time but who don't see the validity of children's ministry? Try exposing the congregation to your children's ministry. Coordinate a Children's Sunday. Put children up front. Create opportunities for kids to lead. Make it known that working in your children's ministry is a *privilege*, not a prison sentence. Help people realize how impressionable children are and how your children's ministry helps them grow into strong Christians.

Another idea is to encourage current volunteers to recruit new helpers. People who are excited about what's happening in your children's ministry can pass on their enthusiasm to others.

One last way to help prospective leaders see the value and fun of children's ministry is to get them started on a part-time basis. Encourage them to fill in for teachers who miss a class or two. Ask them to team-teach for a quarter. If they'll agree to nothing more, ask them to just sit in on a few classes. Maybe the children's warmth and sweetness will convince them.

"I don't want to do what people did to me."

Some potential volunteers recall the emotional bumps and bruises of their own religious training, and they fear that they'll inflict the same educational atrocities on the next generation.

Jane is such a person. As a child, Jane attended Sunday school for only a couple of months. But those few weeks produced decades of bitterness and doubt. Because Jane's family didn't attend church regularly, her church peers were cool toward her when she decided to attend. Yet that rejection seemed small compared to the way the teacher ridiculed her. Jane's teacher humiliated her in front of the class for not knowing all the answers to the Bible questions. One Sunday the teacher even remarked that Jane was stupid. Jane didn't return to church for 20 years.

Though Jane has faithfully attended church for 10 years now, she still carries those vivid images in her head. And though she teaches fourth grade in a public school, she refuses to volunteer in children's ministry. She has tremendous gifts that could be shared with the church children, but she is afraid of inflicting on children the hurt that was inflicted on her.

We can't blame people like Jane for what they feel. But one possible way to draw them in is to encourage them to serve as assistant teachers. Have them work into the program slowly by greeting children, taking attendance, counting the offering, and gathering supplies. Let them observe the ways other teachers interact with children at church and let them see how positive it can be to teach children about God. They may see that this is their opportunity to give today's kids the love, attention, and encouragement that they didn't receive at church.

Another option is to introduce skeptical volunteers to kids through nonthreatening "appetizer" children's activities. Adults can tag along on a fun activity and discover that the children need and even *like* them. This also provides an opportunity for you to check out the ways the prospective leaders interact with kids. If an adult can't have fun with a child, for example, that person may not be ready for children's ministry.

"My child is (or isn't) in the group."

Parents can make excellent volunteers. I especially welcome husband-and-wife teams. Children today need good family role models, and husbands and wives who serve together as group leaders are almost always successful. A husband-and-wife team can keep each other accountable, provide extra creativity, and split the responsibilities. It's a win-win situation.

Some parents want to serve but like to avoid direct interaction with their children. They want their children to learn from other Christian adults. I encourage these parents to get involved with other age groups or to serve as support staff. They can bake cookies, drive kids to a swimming pool, write notes of encouragement to children, and make phone calls.

Some parents won't serve unless they *are* with their children's classes. For most of these parents, serving in their children's classes is a way to spend time with their children and to be involved in the children's spiritual growth. Many parents don't have much time to spend with their children, and the education hour at church becomes a rewarding time for parents and children alike.

A few parents, however, will serve only in their children's classes because they're overprotective—they don't trust others to teach their children. These parents can pose a problem. To deal with them, affirm their desire to protect their children. Then consider talking to them about their tendency to overprotect. Encourage them to allow their children to grow on their own. Finally, encourage the parents to get involved in teaching children other than their own.

The majority of parents make wonderful volunteers. Be cautious, however: Parenthood doesn't automatically qualify a person to be a teacher. We must not look down on anyone who avoids working with children because he or she sincerely doesn't feel qualified. Not everyone has the personality, creativity, energy, or patience to teach children, and some parents accurately recognize their own limitations. Don't make these people feel guilty; affirm them and encourage their involvement wherever they felt comfortable.

"I'm scared!"

Many potential volunteers are genuinely scared to get involved. Sometimes they fear failure. ("What if I can't teach third-graders?") Or they may fear rejection. ("What if they hate me as much as I hated my Sunday school teacher?")

Good training can melt many fears. Too often smaller churches throw frightened, untrained recruits into classrooms. This often produces disaster and discouragement. Teachers who aren't adequately trained will often quit because they feel as if they're doing a bad job. I've found that quarterly (and sometimes monthly) training is common in small churches that successfully recruit and retain workers.

Also, on-the-job training enables new recruits to develop their abilities. Team-teaching is an excellent way to get a hesitant teacher involved. Unfortunately, few small churches incorporate it. They have a hard time finding one teacher, let alone two! But sometimes more people will volunteer if they realize they don't have to do it alone.

"I'll be here forever!"

Many smaller churches take pride in their ability to retain teachers year after year. Unfortunately, some teachers continue to teach because they feel guilty. I've known churches to badger teachers to remain despite their sincere need to take a break. Sometimes volunteers remain on the job because of their loyalty, but those volunteers who are motivated by guilt grow resentful and may become less effective. Shaming volunteers into "till death do us part" service also sends a clear message to potential workers: If you get in, you stay in…for life!

One solution is to define a limited term of service (as short as one month to no longer than one year). Try issuing "Children's Ministry Worker Contracts" (see page 73). Churches that incorporate such contracts usually have fewer recruitment problems. A teacher contract outlines expectations, duties, and standards of conduct. And it often requires that teachers receive some form of training.

I prefer a nine-month teaching contract (September through May). We expect children's workers to give 100 percent during their "contract" months but strongly encourage that they relax during "off-season" months. In the summer we provide alternative programs or recruit temporary help. Then we ask teachers to re-enlist for another nine months. Since workers rarely burn out in a nine-month period, most return for another year.

Stay close to your volunteers. Listen to what they tell you in informal conversations. Talk to their students. You'll be able to tell—sometimes months in advance—whether volunteers will return. Discontented or drained volunteers will send signals that they want out.

Continue to encourage your volunteers even after they've signed their contracts. Express your appreciation often. Be available to answer questions, to locate resources, and to help solve problems. Let volunteers know that their role is not just another job in the church but is a mission to help children learn to know, love, and follow Jesus.

Volunteers will be eager to serve when they feel rewarded. As we strive to present children's ministry as an honorable opportunity within the church, finding volunteers will get easier. Our ministries will benefit if we concentrate on caring for workers and motivating them to stay. Otherwise, we'll always be looking for new people to replace unhappy, exhausted volunteers.

....

1. Les Christie, *Unsung Heroes* (Grand Rapids, MI: Zondervan, 1987), 43-44.

2. Drew Crislip, "Walking a Legal Tightrope With Screening and Training," CHILDREN'S MINISTRY Magazine (May/June 1993), 10.

3. This training video is available for $19.99 from Group Publishing, Inc., Box 481, Loveland, CO 80539. 800-447-1070

CHILDREN'S MINISTRY TRAINING SEMINAR

Use this training seminar to strengthen your volunteer leaders.

Objectives:
- *to build community within a children's ministry leadership team*
- *to discover how common fears in children's ministry can be used as strengths*
- *to discuss how to better teach children*
- *to plan and program a children's ministry calendar*

Time: About 2½ hours

Materials Needed: *Bibles, Bible storybooks, a chalkboard and chalk or newsprint and a marker, a television, a VCR, the video titled* Why Nobody Learns Much of Anything at Church: And How to Fix It, *paper, and pens*

SESSION ONE: What's My Phobia?
(about 45 minutes)

Prior to the training meeting, compile a list of phony phobias that volunteers can easily act out. Possible phobias include smirkophobia (fear of grinning), sneakophobia (fear of athletic shoes), songophobia (fear of singing people), earwaxophobia (fear of earwax), jeanophobia (fear of denim), and hairophobia (fear of hair). The last phobia the volunteers should act out is kidsophobia (the fear of children).

When the children's volunteers have arrived, form four teams. Have each team designate one person as the actor. Tell everyone that the actors are going to be acting out phobias and that their groups are to try to guess what they are acting out. Gather all the actors together and tell them to go back to their groups and act out smirkophobia, the fear of grinning. When all the groups have guessed the phobia, have them choose new actors. Gather the new actors and tell them to act out the next phobia. Continue until all the phobias have been acted out.

Have each small group discuss the following questions.
- **What do people fear in working with children? Which fears are avoidable? Why?**
- **What one aspect of children's ministry do you fear most? Why?**
- **What would help you alleviate this fear?**

continued on next page

Allow 10 minutes for discussion, then bring everyone together. Have the volunteers talk about common fears in children's ministry. Draw a line down the middle of a chalkboard or a piece of newsprint, and write the fears on the left side of the line. Then have people brainstorm possible solutions to each fear, and write the solutions on the right side of the line. Say: **Fear is a common part of being a children's ministry volunteer. Nevertheless, we can learn to trust our instincts, our abilities, and our team to help us overcome fear.**

SESSION TWO:
Why Nobody Learns Much of Anything at Church: And How to Fix It
(about 45 minutes)

Rent or purchase the *Why Nobody Learns Much of Anything at Church: And How to Fix It* video.[3] Show the 30-minute video to your volunteers, then debrief with these questions:

- **Why is Christian education in the local church struggling?**
- **What is one thing you learned from this video?**
- **How will you use this knowledge to be a better teacher?**

SESSION THREE: A Matter of Trust
(about 60 minutes)

Form groups of six or seven volunteers. Have each group form a fairly tight circle with a volunteer standing in the middle. Tell the volunteers in the center of the circles to close their eyes and fall in any direction, keeping their bodies stiff. Have group members catch the people and stand them up again. Let each person take a turn in the center. Then ask:

- **How hard was it to fall into the arms of your ministry team? Why?**
- **Now that you have successfully completed the fall, would it be easier to do it again? Why or why not?**
- **How does this experience parallel the importance of a children's ministry team?**
- **What would you like to trust this team for?**

Keep people in their groups and give groups Bibles and Bible storybooks. Have each group do a brief search in their Bibles and Bible storybooks to identify a time when God's people faced fear or adversity and yet trusted God to get them through it.

continued on next page

Have each group

- record the example/situation (example: Moses and the Israelites at the Red Sea);
- note how the person/people trusted God (example: Moses believed that God would part the waters);
- discover a principle from the story that applies to children's ministry (example: obstacles create opportunities for God to work); and
- develop a brief role play involving an actual children's ministry situation in which this principle comes into play.

After about 15 minutes, have groups perform their role plays for the rest of the volunteers and share the principles they developed. Redirect the volunteers' attention to the fears listed on the chalkboard or newsprint. Ask:

- **How do these principles work in relation to our fears?**
- **Are the principles realistic? Why or why not?**
- **Which principles specifically apply to your own fears about children's ministry?**

Have people remain in their groups, and give each volunteer a note card for each member of his or her group. Have the volunteers write a simple note of affirmation to each of their group members then tape the notes to the clothing of the group members. When each volunteer has had an opportunity to read the affirmations taped to him or her, have the volunteers form one large circle. Close your session with prayer, encouraging volunteers to pray for each other, your children's ministry, and individual children.

CHILDREN'S MINISTRY WORKER CONTRACT

Make two copies of this document. The volunteer worker and the children's ministry director are to sign both copies. One copy is for the volunteer worker; the other should be kept on file at the church.

Name of worker: _____

Position: _____

Period of service: _____

Responsibilities (What will the worker do?)

1.

2.

3.

Expectations (What time commitments and standards of conduct will the volunteer be required to keep?)

1.

2.

3.

Equipping for service (What will the worker receive to increase effectiveness? training-event scholarships? activity reimbursements?)

1.

2.

3.

With God helping me, I will fulfill my responsibilities and expectations in this contract to the best of my ability.

_____
date

_____   _____
children's ministry worker   children's ministry director

Chapter Six

FINDING MONEY

"I know how to live when I am poor, and I know how to live when I have plenty. I have learned the secret of being happy at any time in everything that happens, when I have enough to eat and when I go hungry, when I have more than I need and when I do not have enough. I can do all things through Christ, because he gives me strength"

(Philippians 4:12-13).

Financial issues trouble churches of all sizes, but the smaller church tends to be the hardest hit. According to my research, finding money is the second greatest frustration for small churches.

When funds are limited, it's tough to decide what's really needed for successful ministry and what are unnecessary frills. Some small congregations have learned to discern what they really need and to plan for it, but many others bounce between extravagance and penny-pinching frugality. To boost success, small churches must continually ask, "Is what we're doing the best thing to do? Would other strategies be better or more cost effective?" Smaller congregations just don't have enough money to allow ineffective, tired programs to continue.

We must not forget that our mission is to evangelize, encourage, and equip children to grow in Jesus Christ. Sometimes the wisest financial choice a small church can make is to discontinue an expensive, ineffective program, even if it's a long-standing tradition. At other times, however, the best thing a church can do is to hire additional staff, buy a computer, buy innovative curriculum, or build more classrooms.

It is tough for smaller churches to effectively manage the money they have now, and the future may prove to be even more difficult. The past few decades have revealed a troubling financial trend. Even though personal family income continues to rise, church offerings are decreasing. Since 1968, church income has nose-dived at a cost to church coffers of $2.8 billion. This trend has prompted one research organization to project that many national church structures will become extinct by the year 2048.[1]

What does all of this mean? The smaller church needs to develop coping strategies that provide for successful ministry without financially draining the congregation. Small congregations may also need to learn to be content with fewer programs. In doing so, they might also discover the advantage of doing less but doing it better.

Spending Wisely

A major expense for smaller churches is their children's curricula. Unfortunately, some churches spend far more

"I never thought promising to shorten my sermon would affect the offering."

than is necessary. Many resource rooms in small churches contain unused, dated student papers, extra craft boxes, and dried out, capless markers and glue sticks. Much of this waste may have been avoided through proper ordering and effective resource management.

A children's ministry can save bundles just by thinking ahead. When ordering student books or take-home papers, order enough for the students who attend 75 percent of the time, plus two extra. For example, a Sunday school class roll may contain 15 kids, but perhaps only seven attend regularly. The church should order enough supplies for *nine* children, not 15. Another good idea is to order a curriculum that doesn't rely on student books and take-home papers. The savings will be significant, especially over time.

The only exception is a vacation Bible school program. Since such programs are brief in nature, they require that we "order on faith." Even so, evaluation of past VBS attendance, current children's population, and growth goals can make for a more accurate curriculum order.

It's also vital that smaller churches manage their resources properly. A little preventive maintenance—such as regularly cleaning the heads of the church VCR—will save big bucks later. Cataloging videos and program

10. Use learning materials that can be photocopied. This allows for flexibility when class size changes.

9. To cover costs, charge nominal admission prices ($1 to $2) at parties or special events.

8. Survey the congregation to find special talents (such as clowning, balloon art, and magic) and resources (such as farms, hay wagons, vans, and swimming pools). Use them.

7. Inform parents of special supply requests for items such as paper towels, baby wipes, tissues, and crayons.

6. Hold a "classroom shower." Encourage adults to contribute toys and classroom supplies to the room. Top off the shower with testimonies from the children and refreshments.

5. In a prominent place, post a running list of needs. Encourage congregation members to donate whenever they can. Send thank you notes, signed by the children, to those who contribute.

4. Create homemade postcards from heavy paper and rubber stamps (available through most craft stores). They're less expensive than professional cards, fun to make, and enjoyable to receive.

3. Use restaurant or school playgrounds for activities. Treat the children to sodas at a fast-food restaurant, then let them enjoy the jungle gym.

2. Create your own crafts for VBS and other activities. Craft kits purchased from publishers can cost up to half of a VBS budget. Seek out "crafty" people in your church and encourage them to create simple crafts for the children. Give them plenty of time (at least two months) to develop the craft ideas.

1. Subscribe to CHILDREN'S MINISTRY Magazine. The ideas, programming helps, and encouragement will save money, time, and energy. This magazine pays for itself over and over again.

resources initially takes time. It saves time in the long run, though, because people don't have to spend time searching for missing items. It is important to have markers and glue sticks available to all teachers. Request, though, that teachers take care of the supplies and don't leave them in classrooms so children can play with them and leave them uncovered.

Keep your storage areas and classrooms free from the clutter of used materials. Unless you have a specific plan for their use, outdated curricula should be tossed at the end of each quarter. Reusing teacher packets may be advantageous, but most curriculum publishers make enough minor revisions to each cycle that former teachers guides and student books are obsolete.

See if you can simplify the scope of your program without losing effectiveness. A four-page monthly newsletter is nice, but would a one-page biweekly letter accomplish just as much? Is professionally-delivered pizza necessary, or would frozen or homemade pizza be just as enjoyable?

Sometimes a children's ministry should seek frugal solutions such as the ones mentioned above. At other times, a large expenditure may be a wise investment. For example, a set of children's ministry training videos may seem expensive, but they can be used in many areas of ministry and will "pay off" through more effective leaders. Carefully evaluate every purchase. Look at the staying power of your investment and the effect it will have in the lives of your church's children.

Determining Priorities

Because of cost restrictions, you may not be able to do everything you'd like to do. In such cases, your children's ministry leaders must decide what's most important. You must determine the best allocation of resources, whether you're considering new programs, curricula, or workers' efforts. Sometimes, often to our detriment, such decisions are rooted in tradition. Some small churches won't consider any curricula but the ones published by their own denominations, even if they're the most expensive curricula on the market. Such shortsightedness can bind a church to a program or curriculum that may not be the most effective.

Always remember that programs, philosophies, and resources are only means to an end. Sometimes we need to be flexible and creative and to learn to do without some of the things we want. As Paul encouraged the Philippians to do, we must learn to be content regardless of our circumstances and to trust God to supply for our needs.

Thinking Opportunity

A nearly unlimited bonanza of ministry resources awaits the determined children's worker. To enjoy these resources, the children's worker must be patient, creative, and determined enough to explore every option.

Jim understands this principle. He's a part-time children's-choir director in a church of 90 in the inner city. He wanted to develop a choir of kids from the surrounding urban neighborhood. He hoped to tour with the children and use the choir to introduce more neighborhood kids to Jesus. The problem was money. He had lots of interested kids, the music, and even the support of the parents. But there was little extra cash in the small congregation.

Jim wanted a set of risers for the children to stand on, and he thought a keyboard and a sound system would be nice. A van to transport the children to local performances was important, too. Jim knew exactly what he wanted, and he looked for creative ways to meet the choir's needs.

It didn't take long before his explorations paid off. First Jim discovered that a retired carpenter in his church was willing to build a set of portable risers, donating both his time and the materials. Then, with a few phone calls, Jim located the keyboard and the sound system. A couple of churches were willing to lend them, and one even considered making its loan a permanent donation. A nearby children's home agreed to lend its van to Jim's group as long as basic expenses were covered. Jim's new children's choir was ready to hit the road.

All small churches can find resources as Jim did. It's amazing what's available when you ask for it. Begin with your congregation. Does anyone have the skills or the resources to meet your need? a swimming pool? a computer with a laser printer? entertainment services? professional connections? You'll be surprised at what people will donate if they believe in your work. During VBS, one small church fed hamburgers to over 100 children. The food was donated by a church member who owned a fast-food restaurant. In another church, a bus driver donated both his time and his bus to transport kids.

Auctions and yard sales can be gold mines. Watch for auctions of business or educational supplies. You never know what you'll discover. At one auction, an entire professional lighting set sold for $20. A children's ministry can find educational supplies, audiovisual units, and classroom furniture at such sales.

Local businesses can also help. In many large cities, special warehouses sell bulk items at wholesale prices. You can get huge savings on everything from paper plates to pencils. Furthermore, some businesses are owned and operated by Christians. Many cities now have special Yellow Pages directories that list Christian businesses. Churches shouldn't expect special treatment, but many of these businesses (from print shops to movie theaters) will work with you.

Be willing to pursue all possibilities.

Raising Funds

Fund-raising in children's ministry can be tiring, and it's especially challenging in smaller churches where there are fewer people to contribute. But smaller churches will be successful when they incorporate creative, innovative ideas to raise awareness of their ministry *and* to raise cash.

Here are some sure-fire fund-raisers guaranteed to get the job done in a small church. Each of these ideas is easy to do with just a few children. None of them requires much money upfront, and they're designed to involve adults and children together in ministry. They're *fun,* too.

● **Diving for Dollars**–This is a hot summer fund-raiser that's guaranteed to be "cool" with your children. An outdoor private pool works best (with a good section between 3 and 5 feet deep). Several weeks before the event, encourage adults in Bible classes to contribute silver-colored coins (quarters, dimes, nickels, half-dollars, silver dollars) to a "pool fund."

On the day of the pool event, evenly spread the coins

across the bottom of the pool. Do not allow coins to drop near the pool drain (as they can be sucked in). Give each child participant a plastic cup and have the kids line up around the pool. Signal the children to dive in and retrieve the coins. Give prizes to the top "earners." Another variation is to form teams and have them compete. Either way, this game is a cool way to raise funds. And don't forget the adults. They'll love to watch!

Remember that safety comes first! Don't let too many children jump into the pool at one time—you don't want divers to collide and get concussions.

Ten Fund-Raising Success Secrets[2]

Focus on God's provision through each fund-raiser.

Underline money making with fun!

Nurture kids' growth. Teach kids how to be responsible and to work hard.

Don't limit giving. Suggest a donation, and adults may give more.

Remember to clear all fund-raisers with your pastor.

Arrange for everyone to benefit: the givers and the receivers.

Involve kids.

Schedule fund-raisers around holidays when people are in a giving mood.

Embrace natural opportunities, sponsoring events such as mealtime fund-raisers after services.

Resist overkill. Sporadic fund-raisers are more effective than monthly ones.

• **Pennies to Heaven**—Pennies are often thought of as small, insignificant change. But when added together, pennies can equal big bucks. Over a one-month period, collect pennies from adults and children. Classes might compete against each other (adults vs. adults, children vs. children).

To chart your progress, have contributors trade in their pennies for Bibles. For every 66 pennies collected (one for each Bible book), tape a construction paper Bible to the wall.

The money raised with this fund-raiser can be used to purchase real Bibles for a mission.

• **Pastoral Heights**—Similar to Pennies to Heaven, this fund-raiser uses quarters instead of pennies. The object is for classes or teams of adults and children to create a stack of quarters as tall as the pastor. Since quarters are more valuable than pennies, the earning potential here is far greater than in Pennies to Heaven (especially if your pastor is tall). All quarters become donations to the children's ministry program.

- **Kid Stock**—Kid Stock is an excellent way to raise funds *and* to increase awareness of your program. Print up stock certificates in $5, $10, and $25 denominations. Children sell the stock to interested adults within the church. By buying stock in your children's ministry, people not only provide finances, but also show interest in the children.

Invite every stockholder to a free annual stockholders banquet. At this special event, children cook and serve the meal, provide entertainment, and share their gratitude with each stockholder. The program should also include an evaluation and a survey regarding the children's ministry (during the past year) and a report on what's ahead.

- **Bigger and Better**—Similar to a scavenger hunt, this money maker is guaranteed fun. Give each child in your program one penny. Kids are to find people who will trade nickels for the pennies. Kids then continue to look for people who will trade the next highest denomination. That is, the kids trade pennies for nickels, nickels for dimes, and so forth. They trade $1 bills for $5 bills, $5 for $10, then $10 for $20. The only rules are that any one person may not contribute more than once to one particular child and that each child may contribute only once. It's entirely possible to raise several hundred dollars this way.

- **Super Subs and Soda**—Super Bowl Sunday is an excellent day to sell subs and soda. For several weeks before the big game, have the children give super-sale announcements in worship services and take orders for sandwiches and sodas. Then buy or make submarine sandwiches to fill the orders. Have extra sandwiches on hand for those appetites "made to order" on the day of the game. Set up a booth and have people pick up their sandwiches and sodas after church on Super Bowl Sunday. One small church in Oregon made $200 in sandwich sales.

Another winning combination is muffins and espresso. Adults will have to make the coffee, but children can help set up the booth and sell the muffins. Another twist is to market the sandwiches or muffins for donations only. "Donations only" sales almost always reap larger profits.

● **Wipe a Window**—Here's a fun service project for children to do during a worship hour. You'll need plenty of old newspapers, window cleaner, paper, pens, and envelopes. Simply have the children clean the windows of the cars in your church parking lot. Kids can wipe the side windows while teenagers or adults wipe the front and rear windows.

When the cars are finished, leave notes and small envelopes on them. The note should say something like "Here's looking at YOU! The children of (name of church) need your help, and we've cleaned your windows to help you see our situation better. We're raising money for (name of project) and thought you might welcome the opportunity to contribute! If you are interested, this envelope is provided for your convenience. You may leave your donation at the church office. Thanks! We're here to SERVE you!"

● **Christmas Causes**—Have the children put up and decorate a Christmas tree (for a unique twist, do it in the summertime). On the tree, place small tags that describe needs in your children's ministry. Needs can be small (diapers for the nursery) or large (television monitor). Hang as many tags as possible on the tree. Include programming costs such as summer-camp scholarships, videos for children's church, and a teacher-training magazine.

Encourage families and individuals to each select a tag and purchase the listed item for the church. Keep the tree up for a month and instruct contributors to place their items by the tree. Keep a record of all gifts and send thank you notes to those who give.

● **Money Scavenger Hunt**—Here's a fun Sunday-evening event. Encourage families to come prepared to give (no more than $20). Instruct each family to have its money broken down into small change and just a few $1 bills.

Provide small prizes for the winner of each round, such as packets of flower seeds, boxes of candied popcorn, or plates of homemade cookies.

To play, simply call out an amount of money (for example, $1.62). The family that can produce that amount first wins the round and contributes the money. You can also have families hunt for such things as the oldest coin in the congregation, birthday-year coins, and the dumpiest $1 bill.

Pass the offering plate at the end of the evening and allow families to contribute one last time.

Of course, there are dozens of other excellent fund-raisers: bake sales, candy drives, and subscription sales. But the best fund-raisers are those to which the children give of themselves, their time, or their talents and that challenge adults to take the children's ministry program seriously and to get involved with the kids.

....

1. David Briggs, "Collection Plates Go Begging," *Idaho Statesman* (December 12, 1993), 1F.

2. Christine Yount, "When Your Children's Ministry Needs More Money," CHILDREN'S MINISTRY Magazine (Jan/Feb 1992), 20.

CHILDREN'S MINISTRY BUDGET

A budget for children's ministry helps you to organize your program, establish priorities, and define your overall purpose. Here's a possible financial breakdown for a church of 100 people with 15 children (newborns through sixth grade). This budget encompasses all areas of children's ministry, from curriculum to camp scholarships. A good rule is to budget between $50 and $100 per child per year. This budget of $1100 is a median budget for a church this size ($75 per child per year). You'll also find space to make your calculations and to create a budget for your own children's ministry.

resources/training $475

- music $25   _____
- volunteer training $75   _____
- resource materials $75   _____
- curriculum $300   _____
- other: _____   _____

activities/programming $525

- preschool programming $100   _____
- children's programming $100   _____
- family ministry $125   _____
- children's church $150   _____
- camp scholarships $50   _____
- other: _____   _____

expenses $100

- equipment/audiovisuals $50   _____
- publicity/postage $50   _____
- other: _____   _____

Chapter Seven

TEACHING TO PRODUCE LEARNING

"Watch out and don't forget the things you have seen. Don't forget them as long as you live, but teach them to your children and grandchildren"

(Deuteronomy 4:9b).

All I ever really needed to know I learned...in a small-church Sunday school class. The teachers had few innovative resources. Their classrooms weren't modern in methods and materials. Little teacher training occurred. But teachers worked hard to help children learn the basics of the faith because they were committed to the next generation of Christians.

Some teachers would like to go back to the methods of those days. Unfortunately, we can't go back. The children we minister to today are completely different from the children we were.

Our Changing Children

Children today suffer from sensory overload. Kids are continuously blasted with eye-catching, ear-ringing, nose-tingling attractions. Children are enticed and entertained to excess by everything from computer games to movies. Being a child is different today from the way it was 30 years ago. Today's child travels an information superhighway that was a bike trail 25 years ago. This difference impacts children's ministry for three major reasons.

● **Kids have become an important demographic group to advertisers.** When I was a boy, I collected baseball cards. I knew of only one card company, and half the fun was in chewing the gum packaged with the cards. Today, there are several card companies and most have forgotten about the gum. They pour millions of dollars into coaxing kids to buy their cards. Children are extremely susceptible to the marketing ploys of big companies, and kids are buying those cards like crazy. Some almost drool over the money they think they'll make in a few years after their cards increase in value. Today the fun of baseball cards is in the investment, not in memorizing the stats of favorite players.

"WHAT'S THIS RUMOR I HEAR ABOUT SOME OF YOU SKIPPING MY SUNDAY SCHOOL CLASS?"

Because kids are so courted by today's marketing blitzes, they expect to see some benefit in everything they're asked to do, even if the benefit is just their own personal fun. Thus, teachers and leaders at church must make learning attractive. Children need to see the benefit in going to church. When something gets boring, they'll simply tune it out. And they won't be around long when they see an activity as a waste of time.

● **Family life lends less support.** The changes in the family play a significant role in the change in children's ministry. In many churches, a minority of children live in traditional families with both birth parents. Many are victims of divorce, sexual abuse, or other family dysfunctions. Even "normal" two-parent families are different today because parents are consumed with pursuing careers and earning money. Parents are often absent from kids' lives and sometimes fail to develop the skills (or don't have the energy) to parent properly when they *are* around.

The Sunday school teacher or other group leader often becomes a second parent. The church needs to teach both biblical truth and living skills. The church may be the only place a child can learn important societal guidelines and values. And if parents aren't instilling spiritual values and leading children to Jesus, the people in the church are definitely the only ones who will.

● **Our society is overloaded with opportunity.** And so are the people in our churches. Our teachers and children's workers are drowning in their responsibilities, both inside and outside the church. More women work outside the home, and children and adults alike participate in more extracurricular activities. Consequently, many church commitments are low priorities. It's not unusual for a Sunday school teacher to enter the classroom having spent less than five minutes in preparation!

Children's workers are up against formidable circumstances that make ministry tougher than it's ever been. Smaller churches need to change their teaching strategies or our churches will lose children who find church boring and irrelevant.

Why Few Learn

Christian education faces a crisis. According to the *Yearbook of American and Canadian Churches*, Sunday school attendance has plummeted from 41 million to 32 million since 1972.[1] The 1980s saw a 43 percent decline in the number of churches that offer Sunday school at all.[2] As noted researcher George Barna concludes, "Sunday schools simply do not provide the quality of teaching and experience that people demand these days in exchange for their time."[3]

Sunday school is in trouble. Leading church educators Donald McGavran, Charles Arn, and Win Arn think they know why, and their ideas have implications for the smaller church.[4] First, the focus of the Sunday school has changed from those "outside" to those "inside." Originally, Sunday school was a way to educate unchurched children who worked in factories all week and received no formal schooling or spiritual education. But today, church education is aimed primarily at children who already attend church. Sunday schools don't grow because they're concerned only with the children who are already there.

The loss of community and of a sense of belonging has also contributed to the crisis. "The neighborhood church changed to a 'drive-in' church," suggest the authors. At one time a smaller church was where neighbors met together to worship God, and a strong sense of community developed. But today, people drive to neighboring towns to go to church with people who live in a multitude of neighborhoods. Community spirit is nearly nonexistent. Small churches, in an effort to grow, model their programs after those in larger churches instead of emphasizing their "neighborly" strengths. By doing so, smaller churches reject that natural key to success.

Also, Sunday school has become a low priority within many churches. Pastors are often the only paid staff members in small churches, and many have not been trained in education. Their skills are in preaching and Bible study. Although most pastors believe in strong Christian education programs for children, they're unable to concentrate on building the programs. By the time they take care of the worship service, Bible studies, and the multitude of tasks related to the adult congregation, they have little time left for the children.

All of these things detract from the effectiveness of children's ministry within the smaller church. We are missing the entire mission of the church, which *is* Christian education: "So go and make followers of all people in the world. Baptize them in the name of the Father and the Son and the Holy Spirit. Teach them to obey everything that I have taught you" (Matthew 28:19-20a).

Go, teach, equip—that's Christian education.

As the respected Christian educator Lois LeBar concluded, every church should be "a miniature Bible institute, a laboratory for discovering and implementing eternal truth."[5]

T.E.A.C.H.

So how do we create a stimulating learning environment for children within a smaller church? What strategies should we implement?

I believe the solution is found in the word "T.E.A.C.H.," an acrostic that spells out a description of smaller-church educational effectiveness.

Timely

Christian education should be relevant. Ever hear comments like these?

- "Fifteen years ago we had a packed house in Sunday school…those were the days!"
- "Whatever happened to the time when kids would just sit and listen?"
- "I sure miss my flannel board!"

Times have changed. The small church must recognize that many of its methods are in desperate need of updating. Many adults who teach children are clueless about the world of a child. We sing "Kumbaya" while the kids beat out a rap song. We avoid computers and the children program them. We don't know what it's like to fear for our safety at school, but the kids do. It's vital that we learn about children's everyday experiences to understand their lives and to know what they need from us. The church's strategies must change to meet the needs of the changing child.

Scripture shows us how to be relevant in a changing world without losing the punch of our message. Throughout Scripture, God calls himself "I Am," not "I Was" nor "I Will Be." God touches humanity and interacts with us in the here and now. The smaller church would be wise to do the same. We should constantly be asking, "What can we do *today* to reach children? How can we teach biblical truths relevant to their worlds?" The message of the gospel is timeless, but our strategies must remain timely.

Experiential

People build their lives from experience. Our teaching should help children *discover* for themselves the truths of Scripture through positive personal experience.

Your teaching plans should include as many hands-on, experiential opportunities as possible. Think about what you can do to make lessons come alive. What can your students touch, see, hear, smell, or taste that will bring the point home? Here are a few experiences you could share with your class: Climb a tree and read about Zacchaeus, burrow into a closet and talk about hiding from God, and order hamburgers from a drive-in and give them to a homeless person. Be sure to debrief, showing kids how biblical truth relates to the experiences and to the kids' lives.

Closely related to active, experiential learning is interactive learning. Through small-group discussions and interaction, your kids can learn from each other. They can help one another discover biblical principles that apply to their lives. And they can help one another grow spiritually as they see God at work in each other's lives.

The message of each lesson should become clear through active and interactive learning. Kids should leave your class having felt the lesson, jumped it, heard it, grabbed it, glued it, read it, hugged it, discussed it, thrown it, hammered it, smelled it, torn it, colored it, sang it, acted it, twisted it, and done it period. And the only missing experience should be the one that kids can't wait to come back for next week.

Just Do It!

Group Publishing has done a great job of developing experiential-learning curriculum. Here are just a few resources:

- **Group's Hands-On Bible Curriculum™**–This is available for children ages 2 to 12. Preschool lessons stress one-point learning, puppets, interactive stories, and materials that children can't wait to get their hands on! Lessons for older children employ active learning through the use of wacky "gizmos" that are guaranteed to make every lesson stick. This curriculum is excellent for Sunday school or for any children's meeting. A training video is also available.

- *Sunday School Specials,* **volumes 1 through 3**– Each of these three volumes contains 13 creative programs for multi-grade classes. These lessons make it easy to put kids between the ages of 4 and 12 in the same room. These three books are small-church educational treasures! They are excellent for the summer or any other time when lower attendance demands the combination of children into one multi-grade class.

- *Interactive Bible Stories for Children:* **Old and New Testaments**–Bring those Scripture stories to life! Run from the Egyptians. Fish with Peter. Discover what it was like to be healed by Jesus. The stories are easy to use, and they're great for children's church.

- *Snip-and-Tell Bible Stories* and *Clip & Tell Bible Stories*–Teachers use ready-made patterns to make Bible stories literally unfold for your kids. Teachers tell the stories as they build crafts. These are especially great for younger children who aren't old enough to participate in adult worship or children's church.

- *Lively Bible Lessons* and *Fun-to-Learn Bible Lessons*–These books include topical activities and discussions for children in preschool through third grade. Each book contains 20 age-appropriate lessons that cover faith, family, and personal issues. They're user-friendly, they're fun, and they can be used over and over.

Adaptable

Flexibility is crucial in smaller-church education. You never know what can happen. No matter how well you plan, or how many variables you plan for, surprises abound. Adaptability frees teachers to follow the path the Holy Spirit desires.

Lesson plans are important, but it's OK if you change your plans to fit the needs of your class. When Tim comes to church in tears because his pet rabbit died, you may need to toss aside your lesson plan to respond to the teachable moment. What Tim and the rest of the children can learn from that experience is more important than your lesson plan because it involves real life. The children might learn how to comfort a hurting friend. Tim might learn that God is in control. All of the children can learn about the natural process of life and death and how they fit into God's plan. Tim and the other children will *remember* what they learn from your discussion that morning.

Be prepared for the unexpected. Sometimes the discussion during the opening activity will be so good or the children will ask so many questions that you will never get to the next activity. Remember that the goal of Sunday school is for children to learn about God. The goal isn't for the teacher to get all the way through the lesson.

Also be prepared for times when the lesson just doesn't click with the kids. Take notice when they seem unresponsive or bored. Brainstorm alternative plans in advance, and be ready for such situations. Know before you get to the classroom what you'll do if only one child shows up—or two or even 20. Have backup plans for times when kids aren't doing well with the activities.

Many people think being adaptable means having no plan at all. That's incorrect. Being adaptable means being so well prepared that you have several contingency plans for the *same* lesson.

Creative

Some people are naturally creative, but most people struggle with creativity. The good news is that everyone can *develop* creativity. Try spending time with creative people. You'll be surprised at the way their creativity can rub

Sometimes it's best to combine classes in a smaller church. Lois Keffer, in *Sunday School Specials,* offers the following advice.

● When kids form groups, aim for an equal balance of older and younger kids in each group. Encourage the older kids to act as coaches to help younger students get in the swing of each activity.

● In "pair-share," students work together with a partner. When it's time to report to the whole group, each person tells his or her partner's response. This simple technique teaches kids to listen and to cooperate with each other.

● If an activity calls for reading or writing, pair young nonreaders with older kids who can lend their skills. Older kids enjoy the esteem-boost that comes with acting as a mentor, and younger kids appreciate getting special attention and broadening their skills.

● Don't worry too much about discussion going over the heads of younger students. They'll be stimulated by what they hear the older kids saying. You may be surprised to find some of the most insightful discussion literally coming "out of the mouths of babes."

● Make it a point to give everyone—not just academically and athletically gifted students—a chance to shine. Affirm kids for their cooperative attitudes when you see them working well together and encouraging each other.[6]

off on you. Creativity also comes with practice. You've got an advantage because the smaller church is a tremendous place to practice being creative.

Sometimes you'll make mistakes. I've made a few. I once tried to host a children's swimming party in the baptistery; several responsible women in the church put a stop to that. Under my direction, the children painted the pastor's door shut; the elders frowned and shook their heads. I thought it would be great to sprinkle "prayer dust" (glitter) throughout the worship area as a special prayer; the church janitor disagreed.

When mistakes happen, learn from them. But don't stop being creative. Smaller churches will forgive you for your mistakes just as they forgave me for the ones I made.

The smaller church is also great for creativity because everyone can be involved in the creative process. So what if you don't have Laurence Olivier to lead your children's drama club? You don't need him. You have all the talent and all the creativity you need—in the people who sit in your church's pews every week. The church is creative because God is creative and we're made in God's image. Develop the gift.

Heroic

The final characteristic that marks an effective smaller-church Christian education program is heroism. We should continuously inspire children to become heroes who are more than conquerors.

People tend to live out the expectations others place on them. If we expect children to act up or to disobey, they will. But what if we expect children to become strong, faithful, courageous believers? They'll likely become what we expect them to become.

A lot of kids get lost in large churches. Smaller churches can change the world through the inspiration they give to their children. Small churches can notice the children who limp with emotional and physical wounds. It's hard to lose kids in a small congregation. In fact, it should be impossible.

The heroes are there, right in your classroom. Most of them don't know it yet, and maybe we can't see it, either. But they're there, sometimes with messed up hair, dirty clothes, and nonstop mouths. Each one needs to know that he or she can be a Daniel, a Ruth, or a Solomon. Even if our words of affirmation seem to have little immediate effect, God may use those words to help our church's children become heroes for him.

1. Thom and Joani Schultz, *Why Nobody Learns Much of Anything at Church: And How to Fix It* (Loveland, CO: Group Publishing, Inc., 1993), 8.

2. Schultz and Schultz, *Why Nobody Learns Much of Anything at Church: And How to Fix It*, 8.

3. Schultz and Schultz, *Why Nobody Learns Much of Anything at Church: And How to Fix It*, 9.

4. Charles Arn, Donald McGavran, and Win Arn, *Growth: A New Vision for the Sunday School* (Pasadena, CA: Church Growth Press, 1980), 25-27.

5. Lois LeBar, updated by James E. Plueddemann, *Education That Is Christian* (Wheaton, IL: Victor Books, 1989), 28.

6. Lois Keffer, *Sunday School Specials* (Loveland, CO: Group Publishing, Inc., 1992), 8.

TEACHING TO PRODUCE LEARNING

Ages 3 to 6

Moral Development

Preschoolers are very "me-oriented." They are the center of their own worlds. Their entire view of right and wrong—along with their faith—is based upon what influential models (such as parents and teachers) tell them.

Cognitive Level

Preschoolers' play is symbolic of real life (for example, playing house).

Concepts to Be Learned

- God loves us.
- God made the world.
- God sent Jesus to the world.
- We can love Jesus.

- We go to church to worship God.
- We can help others.
- We can share.
- We can say "thank you."

Teaching Methods and Active-Learning Experiences for Groups of Various Sizes

TEACHING TO PRODUCE LEARNING WITH...	TEACHING METHODS	ACTIVE-LEARNING EXPERIENCES
ONE CHILD	home living art books blocks puzzles music	interactive play book reading neighborhood/nature walks sing-along tapes coloring projects
ONE TO FIVE CHILDREN	home living art books blocks puzzles music	nature walks group story times free play with each other sing-along tapes for worship group coloring projects group paintings modeling-clay sculptures stories on tape
FIVE TO 10 CHILDREN	home living art books blocks puzzles music	group story times group coloring projects modeling-clay sculptures singing and finger plays free play with each other simple crafts learning stations: painting, puzzles stories on cassette group games: Duck, Duck, Goose

TEACHING TO PRODUCE LEARNING

Ages 6 to 8

Moral Development

For younger children, the moral code is "an eye for an eye." If they are pinched, they pinch back. Personal values are rooted in a "law and order" approach. Things that benefit young children are almost always seen as right, whereas harmful things are almost always viewed as wrong. The world, like their faith, is black and white.

Cognitive Level

Young children think in concrete terms about the ideas and concepts they're learning. They need help understanding symbolic or abstract ideas (such as Jesus as the "living water").

Concepts to Be Learned

- *We can make good decisions.*
- *We can talk to God.*
- *We can learn and follow God's ways and commandments.*
- *We can serve Jesus.*
- *God keeps his promises.*

Teaching Methods and Active-Learning Experiences for Groups of Various Sizes

TEACHING TO PRODUCE LEARNING WITH...	TEACHING METHODS	ACTIVE-LEARNING EXPERIENCES
ONE CHILD	art books blocks puzzles music	watercolor paintings modeling-clay sculptures neighborhood/nature walks free play outside reading of simple, beginning books Bible-memory activities sing-along tapes animated Christian videos field trips to parks/restaurants puzzles nature searches with magnifying glass

(continued on next page)

Teaching Methods and Active-Learning Experiences for Groups of Various Sizes *(continued)*

TEACHING TO PRODUCE LEARNING WITH...	TEACHING METHODS	ACTIVE-LEARNING EXPERIENCES
ONE TO FIVE CHILDREN	art books blocks puzzles music	watercolor paintings modeling-clay sculptures neighborhood/nature walks free play outside group reading of simple books group paintings group Bible-memory activities puppet plays crafts small-instrument bands dress-up fashion shows field trips singing
FIVE TO 10 CHILDREN	art books blocks puzzles music	watercolor paintings modeling-clay sculptures organized outside play book centers group Bible-memory activities videotape/audiotape learning centers group puzzles group games: Tag, Red Light/Green Light puppet plays crafts small-instrument bands dress-up fashion shows group singing

TEACHING TO PRODUCE LEARNING

Ages 9 to 12

Moral Development

Children at this age begin to see shades of gray in their world. They question authority more and understand that individual values can impact the lives of others. They also begin to understand that doing "wrong things" (sinning) means more than just "getting into trouble" or facing punishment from parents or teachers. Faith becomes a working, personal faith.

Cognitive Level

Older children continue to think in concrete terms, although by the end of childhood they can more readily understand abstract concepts.

Concepts to Be Learned

- *We can live for God in today's world.*
- *We can understand the elements of the Christian faith.*
- *The church is important.*
- *We can improve relationships with our families and peers.*

Teaching Methods and Active-Learning Experiences for Groups of Various Sizes

TEACHING TO PRODUCE LEARNING WITH...	TEACHING METHODS	ACTIVE-LEARNING EXPERIENCES
ONE CHILD	art drama music creative writing oral communication outreach opportunities community builders	research projects (using Bible commentaries) arts and crafts field trips/tours letters to missionaries/ pen pals simple science experiments cooking/baking write a play, song, etc.

(continued on next page)

Teaching Methods and Active-Learning Experiences for Groups of Various Sizes *(continued)*

TEACHING TO PRODUCE LEARNING WITH...	TEACHING METHODS	ACTIVE-LEARNING EXPERIENCES
ONE TO FIVE CHILDREN	art drama music creative writing oral communication outreach opportunities community builders	research project (Bible commentaries) arts and crafts field trips/tours letters to missionaries/pen pals group science experiments group cooking/baking dramatic/puppet presentations videotaping of Bible stories/parables Bible-memory activities/games writing of plays, songs, etc.
FIVE TO 10 CHILDREN	art drama music creative writing oral communication outreach opportunities community builders	research projects in teams age-appropriate crafts missionary-support projects team science experiments group dramatic/puppet presentations videotaping of Bible stories/parables children's choir writing of plays and songs

Chapter Eight

EFFECTIVE PROGRAMS

"I have become all things to all people so I could save some of them in any way possible. I do all this because of the Good News and so I can share in its blessings"

(1 Corinthians 9:22b-23).

A smaller-church children's minister is often like a plate spinner at the circus who spins a dish on top of a pole. Then another dish. And another. Eventually, the exhausted performer does little else but run from pole to pole, giving each plate a fresh spin.

Then a dish slows to a wobble and...*crash!*

Children's programs can be just as hard to keep going. Many programs wobble in mediocrity, spun halfheartedly because there are simply too many programs. A widely diverse ministry seems attractive, but it poses problems for the performers, who in the smaller church are overworked volunteers. Spinning too many program plates may lead to pessimism, apathy, and financial struggles.

Still, cutting a program may seem next to impossible. We've been trained to believe that expansion is success; thriving churches *add* programs—they don't cancel them. However, few things are eternal. We must remember that all programs (Sunday school and VBS included) are merely strategies for ministry. Strategies must change as people change. When a program isn't bringing children closer to God, we must change it, cancel it, or rest it for a while.

Don't misunderstand my point. We need programs. After all, a program can attract children or help them grow spiritually. It can bring in families. We just need to realize that programs are tools for building the body of Christ. We don't necessarily need *all* of the programs other churches have. A lot of small churches are convinced, however, that abandoning programs would mean the collapse of the churches.

For smaller-church children's ministries to survive and thrive, those involved need to evaluate *every* program with several well-targeted questions: Why do we offer this program? Is the program getting the job done? Is it cost-effective? Is there a better way to get better results? Do we provide this ministry because someone else does, because it's church tradition, because it's part of someone's agenda, or because it's the best program we can offer?

We must never lose sight of our goal in children's ministry: to help children learn to love and follow God. Every program we offer needs to lead children along on the journey of faith. This chapter examines a few programs that reach kids. It provides ideas and encouragement for specific ministries. But pick and choose carefully. The answer to children's ministry in a smaller church is not always to add *another* program. Go back to Chapter 4 and see what the focus of your ministry is. Then choose only what will work with your children in your church with the resources you have.

Programs That Reach New Children

Every children's program must be focused outward. Even activities developed to strengthen the faith of church kids must turn them toward reaching out to others. Sunday

Thanks to the summer slump,
Pastor Butterman was finally able
to try his hand at
intergenerational ministry.

school should encourage children to actively incorporate biblical principles into their lives. Worship should inspire kids to love God Monday through Saturday as well as on Sunday. And other activities should be designed specifically to attract unchurched children.

The following programs can draw in new children. And they can help children within the church to personally reach out to others.

Choir, Drama, and Puppet Groups

These programs are excellent tools for ministry. In one small church, a pastor's wife recruited a group of five children who were interested in music. Within weeks, her choir had grown to 10 kids and was contributing special music to worship services monthly. The children ranged in age from 3 years to 12. That church of 60 people had never seen anything like it before. And while the children were hardly a polished choir, they motivated everyone to sing with a smile.

Use these tips to help your group succeed:

- **Involve the children.** Let them help choose the music or the script. Also, have them think of a name that reflects the purpose of your group. Write encouraging notes to the children. Do a group-building activity before each practice.

- **Involve parents.** Mom and Dad are vital to the group's success. Encourage parents to be involved. They can videotape performances, organize fund-raisers, transport children, and provide refreshments. Be thorough when communicating to parents what you need from them. Provide dates, times, and any other relevant information. Give them plenty of notice when you expect their help.

- **Be organized.** If you aren't leading the group, appoint one person to be in charge. The person in charge should be prepared and on time for each rehearsal. He or she should study the music or scripts in advance and have a contingency plan in case things don't go as planned. The leader should also have an up-to-date list of all group members and their parents' names, phone numbers, and addresses.

- **Work toward a performance.** The best motivation for kids is the chance to perform for others. Schedule one performance and start small. You might have the children perform for a Sunday-night service or an adult Sunday school class. When the kids have successfully pulled off one performance, you can easily schedule more.

- **Aim for excellence.** Never perform before you're ready, but don't wait for perfection. Obtain a commitment from the children to be at practices, but always be understanding of circumstances beyond their control. Inspire kids to improve their skills. Be excited—children will respond to your excitement. And they'll respond to the compliments that their well-rehearsed performance brings.

A small church in Colorado developed an annual children's musical that attracts people from throughout the community. Each year, the production is just a bit better. And each year more people are exposed to the ministry of this congregation. Plus, finding volunteer help is practically a snap. Adults want to be involved in the successful program.

Kids' Clubs

Kids' clubs are usually established weekly programs with set curriculums, such as Royal Rangers, Pioneer Clubs, and Awana. Some churches create their own kids' clubs based on the specific needs of their kids and on the abilities of their volunteers. Creating a program is often the best solution for a smaller church because everything can be tailored to the exact situation. However, creating a weekly program requires a significant amount of time and organization.

Before you add a kids' club to your ministry, think about these questions:

● How does this program promote Christian growth?

● Does this program fit my children's ministry philosophy?

● Is the timing of the program right?

● Is the program fun for both children and their parents?

● Is this program geared to reach children beyond the church or, at the least, prepare churched kids for evangelism?

A lot of kids' club programs fail too many of these criteria. Furthermore, some programs are quite expensive or demand lots of volunteers.

Numbers also play a role in the decision to develop a kids' club. If fewer than 10 children will regularly be a part of the kids' club, consider postponing your plans. Such small groups can flourish, but more often, groups with fewer than 10 kids struggle to stay alive.

The age span of your children is important, too. A lot of kids' clubs use games and activities that make incorporating a wide age-range difficult. Furthermore, a primary purpose of a kid's club should be to attract other children into your children's ministry. Persuading older, unchurched children (especially fifth- and sixth-graders) to participate in a program with kindergartners will be difficult.

After-School Programs

After-school programs are excellent ways to reach children. Such programs meet the needs of children who otherwise would go home to empty houses because their parents work. If your church is located near an elementary school, attracting kids will be easy. Even if it isn't, your program can be effective.

Begin by asking: "What needs can we meet through this program?" "Is the program in line with our church's philosophy?" "How often will we offer the program?"

You might start by inviting schoolchildren once a week. Publicity is essential to attracting both children and parents. Elaine Friedrich, a Texas children's worker and director of a successful after-school program, also suggests that you determine what grades of children can participate in the program, what the schedule will be, and how to meet any transportation needs.[2] You may not be able to do all you'd like to, but emphasize what you can do and develop a solid program.

Most after-school programs operate for $1\frac{1}{2}$ or two hours in the afternoon immediately after the school day. Often parents will pick up children at the church on their way home from work. Placing a donation container by the door may help you meet expenses.

Provide a variety of activities: Play games, build crafts, read Bible stories, and watch videos. You may want to arrange to have adults tutor children. Provide a light snack because many of the children will eat dinner late. Keep the structure of the program fairly loose and give the children options. Allow the program to breathe with as much creativity as possible, given the restrictions of volunteers, time, and finances.

Some smaller-church leaders may object to unchurched kids or children from other churches using your church's property and supplies. But we must remember our purpose. As Paul said in 1 Corinthians 9:22-23, we must attempt to reach all people—even those outside our congregation—and teach them about Jesus. It's sad when a church building (large or small) sits vacant day after day as hundreds of children pass by. Think of the opportunities missed!

Backyard Bible Studies

Backyard Bible studies are another excellent form of outreach. These satellite children's groups require little money and minimal volunteer support. For one backyard

Bible study, you need only a home with a spacious yard and one parent/volunteer.

A backyard Bible study is small by nature. The 10-children minimum for kids' clubs doesn't apply here. Backyard Bible studies can be effective with as few as three children. Unless there's ample room, a group should not exceed 15 children.

A backyard Bible study is an excellent smaller-church children's program for several reasons. It's less threatening than meeting in a church building, so it's easier to invite friends. It's convenient and close; parents usually don't have to drop their children off. It's cost-effective. For example, many homes already possess materials—such as playground balls, basketball hoops, televisions, VCRs, and pools—for entertainment and teaching times. Unchurched parents are more likely to let their children attend an event at a neighbor's house than one at the church.

A backyard Bible study shouldn't last longer than two hours. A possible evening schedule might look like this:

6:30 p.m.—games
7:00 p.m.—cool down and snack
7:15 p.m.—Bible study/lesson
7:45 p.m.—craft time
8:10 p.m.—affirmation and prayer time
8:30 p.m.—head for home

For materials, some churches use extra lessons from 10-day vacation Bible school curricula. Others incorporate topical studies. Crafts are excellent, especially for those children who are not interested in the games. The key is to be flexible.

Backyard Bible studies work with all ages, even preschoolers. Moms who come with their preschool children welcome adult conversation and the opportunity to focus on similar concerns and problems. A backyard Bible study for mothers of preschoolers, with creative activities for the children, will be attractive in many neighborhoods. It can also attract new families to your church. Many small churches have adapted the popular national program Mothers Of Pre Schoolers (MOPS). These weekly meetings provide support for harried mothers and social interaction for young children. While most MOPS groups meet in churches, a home could work just as well.

Summer Ministry

Many churches wind down to "rest" during the summer. The rationale seems reasonable: The weather is hot, everyone's busy, and people are gone on vacations. However, children are the most available during the summer—they have lots of free time. And summer programs can be exciting!

In many ways, summer is the perfect time for smaller-church children's ministry. In comparison to large groups, small groups of children are easier to manage during fun activities such as trips to the zoo and to the swimming pool. Unfortunately, small churches can get tripped up when they're planning more formal programming. Try the ideas that follow to help make your summer programs more fun and more effective.

Vacation Bible School

For the last 100 years, VBS programs have helped thousands of children grow closer to God. And VBS programs have changed many times to meet the needs of new generations. Today, many people are saying that traditional VBS is old-fashioned and painfully obsolete. Many churches—large and small—have abandoned this summer program.

Some suggest that VBS no longer meets needs. Some say the format is outdated. Some say a daily schedule is too demanding for families struggling to find more time for each other. Others claim that VBS no longer focuses on its original purpose of evangelism. In most churches, it's just a "church kid" program.

Some of these criticisms are valid. But children still need to learn about God, and VBS is a great way for kids to have fun and grow spiritually. The small church can easily change formats to make VBS a strong and vital part of a children's ministry.

Gospel Light curriculum publishers suggest these fun alternatives to traditional VBS.[3]

● backyard Bible clubs—Head for the neighborhoods. Meet five days in a row or one day per week for five weeks.

● day camp—Gather at the church each day during one week. Then travel to a park, camp, or farm.

- Terrific Tuesdays (or Wacky Wednesdays)—Choose one day per week during the summer to meet or do something special.
- the three-three-three plan—Because many families take mini-vacations on long weekends, hold VBS for three hours on Tuesday, Wednesday, and Thursday for three weeks.
- family nights—Meet one night each week of the summer and use programming for intergenerational groups.
- children's church—Use a VBS curriculum in your Sunday-morning program for the summer.
- family camp—Schedule family events during the evenings of one week so moms and dads can come.
- VBS split—Plan a two-week VBS, but hold sessions in the daytime during the first week and in the evening during the second week.
- split season—Plan VBS for winter or spring breaks. This works well with year-round school schedules.
- all day Saturday—Have a big event on a Saturday from 9 a.m. to 7 p.m. People can come and go, or they can stay for the entire day.

Smaller churches can also join forces with other small churches in the area to offer a single VBS program. Some do this within their own denomination, but others have coordinated programs interdenominationally. The event can be on neutral territory, such as a public park, or it can be at a larger church building that can accommodate crowds. The pooling of teachers and resources is a definite advantage.

One more twist on VBS is to hold a weekend event Friday through Sunday. One church has even moved the program out of the hectic summer schedule and created a joint VBS/fall kickoff event known as "Celebrate!" The program, which features activities for kids of all ages, begins on Friday night and runs through Sunday. On Sunday night, the event closes with a traditional fall kickoff at the YMCA. And since it's held the weekend after Labor Day, it has little competition.

Summer Camps/Day Camps

Many denominations already provide organized camps for children. However, some of these camps are expensive or distant. A possible solution is to organize a one-day camp for your children. The camp can meet during the week or on a Saturday. And it can be held almost anywhere, from the churchyard to a nearby national park. Be sure to schedule plenty of outdoor exploration time. Observe wildlife and talk about God's creation. Play lawn games or water games. Provide snacks and lunch. Build crafts. End the day with camp songs and a short devotion or prayer time.

Another option for the smaller church is a family-style camp. Many churches have great success with such camps. Families are responsible for their own campsites, including meals. However, corporate worship and devotional times can be offered as well as other programs such as nature walks, creative Bible lessons, fishing, and swimming.

Day Trips

Summer is a great time to get out and experience area attractions such as water parks and zoos. Day trips can be sizzling summer fun. Ask your local chamber of commerce for a schedule of special summer activities (such as parades and circuses) and unique getaways (such as children's days at local attractions). Don't be afraid to probe. Longtime residents can be tremendous resources. Keep a file of all the creative, fun activities available in your area.

Check out these 14 attractions that won't tax your time or your pocketbook:

- swimming pools—either public or private
- area food factories
- radio or television stations or newspaper offices
- petting zoos, farms, city zoos
- natural history museums, planetariums
- historical museums, historical tours, ghost towns
- fishing at a city lake, a pond, or a stream
- tours by bus, carriage, or train
- mountain picnics, city-park lunches, or ocean-beach snacks
- amusement parks or water parks

- minor league baseball games, county fairs, kids' rodeos
- bowling, roller-skating, video arcades
- $1 movies
- digging for fossils, panning for gold, hunting for insects

You can give a creative twist to many of these activities by simply combining two or more into a single activity. Go on an "insect" scavenger hunt. Hold a swimming pool "rodeo" (with such activities as tube riding and races). A day trip can last for as little as an hour or as long as the whole day. Keep in mind that longer trips are best for older children.

Bible Studies

Summer also provides an excellent opportunity for special Bible lessons. Focus on active learning in special locations. Create experiences where Bible stories come to life. Sit at the beach and review the Red Sea experience. Plant a garden and discuss spiritual growth. Tour a courtroom and study God's justice. Walk in a wheat field and explore the parable of the wheat and the weeds.

Try creating project-oriented Bible study programs. One children's ministry developed a Creation museum (after a study of Genesis). The museum featured fossils, bones, and dinosaur replicas. Kids can also paint murals, develop dramas, or create musicals.

Intergenerational Ministry

Children and older adults benefit from contact with each other. A smaller church can develop a strong intergenerational program simply by creatively connecting children with older adults. Older adults have a wealth of knowledge, skills, and love to share with children. Have children serve snacks to older adults at a Bible study. Pair up older adults and children at a picnic or a banquet. Invite older adults to teach children skills like baking cakes or building birdhouses.

Interaction between children and older people can benefit the other generations as well. My daughter Becca loves games and will play them for hours. Some days my wife and I are simply gamed out. But Becca has found some older ladies in our neighborhood who will play games with her, and they never tire of her energy. Furthermore, Becca teaches these unchurched ladies the songs and stories she's learned in Sunday school. In fact, she may be the only Jesus they see all week. Everyone wins!

---

1. Jolene L. Roehlkepartain, ed., *Children's Ministry That Works!* (Loveland, CO: Group Publishing, 1991), 151.

2. Elaine Friedrich, "Ten Strategies for Launching an After-School Program," CHILDREN'S MINISTRY Magazine (March/April 1991), 14-15.

3. "VBS Alternatives," CHILDREN'S MINISTRY Magazine (March/April 1994), 19.

Chapter Nine

CHILDREN AND WORSHIP

"But Jesus said, 'Let the little children come to me. Don't stop them, because the kingdom of heaven belongs to people who are like these children'"
(Matthew 19:14).

Janie is the type of kid who would get lost in a big church. But in her church, she has an important role that came about one Sunday during the worship service.

It was a sweltering August Sunday, and Janie was only 5 years old. Nothing unusual happened until 25 minutes into the message. As the pastor began his final point, his voice cracked. Within seconds he was coughing so hard that tears formed in his eyes.

The moment the pastor began coughing, Janie was gone. She ran to the church kitchen and asked for a glass of water because she was too small to reach the faucet. A moment later Janie bounded onto the platform and shyly handed the pastor the water.

The grateful pastor drank every drop. Then he unveiled his third point: "I tell you the truth, whoever gives you a drink of water because you belong to the Christ will truly get his reward" (Mark 9:41).

Janie hasn't missed a Sunday since.

After that service, the pastor asked Janie if she'd bring him a glass of water every week from then on, and Janie beamed. "No pwoblem," she replied. Every Sunday, there's a fresh glass of cool water on the podium.

From time to time, especially when the temperature soars, the pastor will recount the story of the day Janie gave the water. And no one seems to mind hearing the story again.

Children in Adult Worship

To this day, Janie is excited about worship because she knows it relates to her. Children can feel as if they belong in adult worship services if the services are geared in some way toward them. A kid-friendly worship service will include songs, devotional thoughts, or a special message that children will understand. And whenever possible, children should be involved in the service.

Sadly, almost all adult worship experiences are created by adults, for adults. During the service, from the music to the message, kids are usually ignored or told to be quiet. Kids *do* learn, even in the most formal and adult of all worship services. But what they usually learn is that worship is for adults, is boring, and is too complicated for them to understand.

Worship doesn't have to be that way. The smaller church can create kid-friendly services more easily than the large church can. A small congregation has more room for kids to participate. The flexibility of a small church provides a more comfortable atmosphere for children's first tries at leadership. And the community spirit in smaller churches makes for less embarrassment when children make mistakes.

To involve children more fully in your worship services, first consider the children in your congregation. What are their gifts? interests? abilities? How can you use those gifts during a worship service? When I was 10 years old, my

It's not that tough to make sermons more kid-friendly. But first, get to know your church's children. Interview them about their hobbies, interests, foods, television shows, favorite music, and sports heroes. Eat pizza with them and watch a movie or a hit TV show they'll enjoy. Play a game of basketball. Discuss their heroes. Then you'll be better prepared to use these ideas that even your adults will probably enjoy.

● **In each message, use at least one illustration that children will understand.** Don't know if a story will work? Try it out on a few fourth-graders first. Do you want a point to be meaningful for kids? Illustrate it with objects, articles, and situations from a child's world.

● **Create sermon-time games.** Make up Bingo cards with thoughts from the week's sermon. Encourage the children to listen for the thoughts and to mark them. Have them bring their cards and explain the thoughts the following week. Or give older children a chance to summarize your sermon at the end.

● **Use objects to explain points.** A sermon about the Light of the World? Preach by candlelight. Talking about sin? Deliver your message beside a garbage can of smelly trash. Or get a haircut as you tell the story of Samson.

● **Watch your language.** Leave your dictionary at the door. "Propitiation" and "sanctification" sound scholarly, but children—and quite a few adults—will be clueless about your point. If you are referring to something in Greek or Hebrew, be sure to explain it in simple terms.

● **Use children's names and stories.** Listen for humorous family anecdotes and interject them whenever possible. Parents love to hear the stories, and kids enjoy the personal attention. If the material is sensitive, get permission first.

● **Make personal applications for children.** Talking about giving? Encourage children to tithe on their allowances. Teaching about loving enemies? Help kids realize that this includes the mean kids at school. Denouncing idol worship? Apply the lesson to electronic games, sports, or television stars.

● **Let children help give the sermon!** Have children hold props, participate in illustrations, teach object lessons, or act out Bible stories.

"You should get a halo! That would look awesome!"

doodling in church eventually landed me a "chalk talk" opportunity. In front of the entire congregation, I drew a pastel picture as the preacher spoke of a Christian's hope. The picture wasn't a masterpiece, but it hung in the basement of that church for years.

Another strategy for involving kids is the children's sermon. Some churches do this weekly and others monthly. Children gather around the minister or another adult who shares a brief lesson for children. One small church placed a couple of caterpillars in jars and checked on them weekly until butterflies came out of the caterpillars' cocoons. The pastor related the experience to how a person can be a new creation in Jesus.

A different children's-sermon idea is a "sermon in the sack." Each week a different child brings an object hidden in a paper sack. The children gather and the article is revealed. Then the minister—who didn't know what the object was in advance—must somehow connect a spiritual truth to the object. It's unpredictable, fun to watch, and educational.

Children can also be involved through music and drama. Few things bring more smiles than a child's toothless rendition of "Jesus Loves Me." And puppets bring out the kid in everyone. Use puppets to "mouth" a contemporary Christian song, introduce the pastor, or even give an announcement.

Twenty-Five Ways Children Can Serve in the Church

Children need not wait until they're older to take an active role in the church. Here are some creative, helpful ways they can serve *now!* Think about the children in your group and write potential names beside each task.

1. Select hymns for Sunday worship.
2. Serve on the children's ministry planning committee.
3. Assist in the church nursery (with an adult).
4. Write a children's column for the church newsletter.
5. Photocopy, fold, and/or collate the church bulletin or other church materials.
6. Serve as a greeter at worship services.
7. Vacuum the church worship area or do other cleaning.
8. Light candles.
9. Read the Scripture text.
10. Adopt a "compassion child" and raise necessary funds.
11. Write letters to church-supported missionaries.
12. Work with an adult to develop a devotional to read during the offering.
13. Play an instrument for the singing time during the worship service.
14. Operate the slide projector or overhead projector.
15. Lick and stick stamps for church mailings.
16. Visit a nursing home with an adult.
17. Adjust all the church clocks to daylight-saving time.
18. Create cards and deliver them to a children's medical ward.
19. Take up the offering or distribute bulletins.
20. Catalog and shelve books in the church library.
21. Create a poster for a church event.
22. Offer a prayer before an all-church potluck.
23. Cut out and post newspaper clippings featuring church members.
24. Plan a church social.
25. Lead an activity for a younger group.

Worship is more kid-friendly when you use overhead transparencies instead of hymnals and when you use maps, pictures, and objects to illustrate the message. For example, bring a picture of the arid country of the Middle East when the message is about living water and bring a slingshot when the message is about David and Goliath. Before or after the service, allow the children to handle the slingshot or get a better look at the picture.

Children (as well as many unchurched adults) may be confused by church rituals or traditions. Explain difficult concepts creatively. A church in Boise, Idaho, 35 members strong, does an annual Living Last Supper portrayal to teach the congregation and guests the possible thoughts of disciples on the night prior to Jesus' crucifixion. An event that's often just a picture in a book comes to life for the children.

Consider using a video to involve kids in worship. Videotape kids as they respond to the question "What does God look like?" and replay the videotape as an introduction to a sermon about God's nature. Show a zoo video as the pastor praises God for creation.

You can also use older children as readers and ushers. Children can hand out bulletins, greet worshipers, and collect the offering. Older children can read short, inspirational stories or announcements for coming events. Kids can read Bible passages, responsive readings, or letters from missionaries. Even young children can recite verses they've learned. If you ask children to read something in worship, give them the material well in advance. Encourage them to practice the reading in the sanctuary. This kind of involvement not only exposes children to leadership in a congregation and provides experience, but also helps them learn to speak in public.

Many of these ideas will make your adult worship services more comfortable for children. But adult worship may not meet all of children's worship needs. And that's where the concept of children's church fits in.

Children's Church—Making It Work

Children's church can build your children's ministry and encourage spiritual growth in kids who might otherwise get lost. Children's church usually runs during the same hour as adult worship. That means it's prime time children's ministry, since some families come for only one hour. Children's church may be the only time all week you'll see certain kids.

To determine if your children's ministry could benefit from children's church, first look at the number of children in your church. The 10-children rule applies here. If your church has fewer than 10 children between first grade and fifth grade, a children's church will probably struggle. It's too hard to excite fewer than 10 children about singing and other group worship activities. Children simply feel too self-conscious to sing out if there aren't a lot of other kids present. If you have just a few children, it may be better to emphasize involving children in adult worship.

What's the Purpose?

Children's church is more than a fun-and-games hour. It has a higher purpose than keeping noisy kids out of the adults' way. The purpose of children's church is to help kids learn to praise and worship God. It won't work to pattern children's church after adult services because children worship differently. Kids need to explore the wonders of God, using all their senses. Then they need to have fun praising God.

Children's church should also prepare kids for adult worship experiences. In other words, an effective children's church will help children understand confusing aspects of adult worship. It will explain the lyrical content of hymns and the meaning of events like baptism and communion. Children's church will also teach children to understand "worship etiquette," defining the basic rules of worship in the church's tradition.

Tips for Success

Children's church frustrates many smaller churches. Almost six out of 10 small churches I surveyed gave their children's church programs a grade of C or below. The struggles included ministering to children of many different ages, creating excitement and consistent attendance, and finding volunteer support.

The following tips will help you develop a successful children's church program.

● **Make the program relevant.** Outdated curriculum and campfire songs from 1968 won't cut it. Today's child is assaulted daily by advertising from companies that clearly understand kids. Churches need to make programs relevant to today's children.

To understand today's children, find out what attracts them. Watch after-school or Saturday-morning television and pay particular attention to the commercials. Interview your kids to see what music they like and what movies they enjoy. Spending time with children will broaden your perspective of their world.

One good option is to use good videos. Christian videos continue to improve in quality and quantity. Just be careful not to overuse them. If you show them more than twice a month, they'll become tiresome.

● **Personalize your children's church.** Create an atmosphere where children get to know each other. Sprinkle your programs with creative mixers and affirmation exercises. Also, recognize the danger in working with a wide age span. Many smaller-church children's worship programs include kids as young as 3 and as old as 12. That's too wide a span. A good span, providing you have 10 participants, is from first grade to fifth grade. Give sixth-graders the option of attending adult or children's worship (most will choose the adult service). If possible, have a separate program for preschoolers and kindergartners. They struggle among older children.

Resource Spotlight:

101 Creative Worship Ideas for Children's Church

Children's ministry can be frustrating, especially when you've drained the well of ideas. *101 Creative Worship Ideas for Children's Church,* by Jolene Roehlkepartain, provides age-appropriate, easy-to-prepare ideas for active worship and prayer. This book includes devotions, object-lessons, Bible stories, puppet scripts, holiday ideas, and more. The book also provides five ready-to-go bonus worship services. *101 Creative Worship Ideas for Children's Church* is loaded with suggestions that will spark singing, prayer, movement, and worship in your children's church. This valuable resource is available through Group Publishing.

Also, during teaching times, it's wise to further divide your elementary children into two groups: first through third grade and fourth and fifth grade. Have all the children worship together. Sing several songs, listen to a brief missions presentation, and take an offering. Then form more age-appropriate groupings for teaching and affirmation. Small groups of same-age peers invite better participation and allow for more personal attention. Again, such group dynamics are not always possible in a smaller church, so it's wise to evaluate your situation before you leap in with both feet.

Many other strategies help personalize children's church. Provide name tags. Remember birthdays. Encourage children to pray for each other by name. Play name games. Display a city map with a pin designating the location of each child's home. Send notes to sick or absent children.

● **Make children's church active.** Sing lively worship songs and encourage movement. Create experiential offerings: Children must leave their seats to give their money. Use active learning: If you're teaching about the feeding of the 5,000, serve fish crackers and tuna on the church lawn. Want to study Job's patience? See which child can suck on a piece of candy-covered chocolate the longest. Keep the activities moving. An attention span for an elementary child lasts 5 to 15 minutes at best.

● **Provide opportunities for children to lead.** Encourage children to take on any tasks or roles that they can handle. They can operate an audiocassette or videocassette player, give a devotion during the offering, say a prayer, lead songs, flip transparencies, distribute handouts or art supplies, set up chairs, collect the offering, read Scripture, share personal testimonies, sing songs, read announcements, or clean up the worship area.

You can also infuse your children's church with "mission-mindedness" and emphasize whole-church ministry. Write letters to missionaries. Support a Compassion International child. Send a care box to children in an orphanage. Bake cookies for people in a nursing home. Create cards for sick children. Or paper the pastor's office with appreciation notes.

● **Have consistent leadership.** Children welcome routine as long as it's not dull. Try to maintain a steady program. Constant turnover of adults, repeated changes in the format, and inconsistent disciplinary procedures will erode even the best of children's church programs. The smaller-church problem is obvious. Who's going to commit week in and week out to children's church, especially if it meets simultaneously with adult worship?

One idea that makes finding leaders for children's church easier is to develop a Family Sunday. Once a month, cancel children's church so the children and leaders can worship with the adults. Children get to see adults in worship, and families can worship together. On Family Sunday, allow children to participate in some way, such as singing a special music song.

Another option is to lessen the amount of commitment from workers. Instead of recruiting three volunteers for the entire hour, why not recruit a song leader, a missions leader, and a teacher? Instead of sacrificing the entire hour, the song leader and the missions leader are involved only for a ten- to fifteen-minute segment, after which they can return to adult worship. Many adults welcome this type of commitment.

Try involving teenagers in leading parts of children's church. Young people can be great worship leaders for children. Teenagers enjoy leadership roles and can make effective teachers under adult supervision.

Also, don't be afraid to cancel children's church during demanding months. Summer is almost always tough, and December is, too—especially during the last two weekends. Anytime you can give volunteers a break, you'll be developing loyalty.

● **Keep the format consistent.** Children's church should also be fairly consistent in format. This schedule may work for your church.

10:30 to 10:45—songs and praise
10:45 to 10:50—offering
10:50 to 11:00—missions moment
11:00 to 11:20—Bible lesson: activity and discussion
11:20 to 11:30—share and care/affirmation time
11:30 to 11:40—prayer circle

Specific activities differ each week, but the schedule remains firm. Why? Because children are comfortable with order. Does that rule out spontaneity? Certainly not. If an activity doesn't work, move on. If a teachable moment occurs, be sure to pursue it. If you have a special guest who can keep kids interested in something of spiritual value for most of the hour, take advantage of it. For the most part, however, stick to the routine.

● **Be consistent with discipline.** Discipline is often another frustration for children's church workers. Smaller churches generally have an advantage in that there are fewer children than in larger churches. Often the more children you have, the more problems you have.

First of all, it's a good idea to have written children's church behavior guidelines. Make copies for all the parents. Post the guidelines in the meeting room. Then the kids will know the guidelines, and so will the parents.

Try to write guidelines in a positive manner. For example, "Don't talk when the teacher or another student is speaking" is a poorly worded guideline. A better guideline is "If you have something to say, raise your hand and wait to be called on. Speak only that which is good, is helpful, and builds up others."

The important thing is to communicate the expectations and then be willing to carry them out. Kids can tell rather quickly if the rules are made to be broken.

You can avoid a lot of discipline problems if you understand why children become disruptive. There are essentially two reasons. First, the unruly child may desperately need attention. He or she will stop at nothing to get it. Unfortunately, even negative attention is better than none. The solution is to affirm such kids for good behavior whenever you can. Encourage positive behavior and try to ignore negative actions. You'll soon see a change.

Second, the child has never been taught appropriate behavior guidelines. Spend time helping such children understand what are appropriate actions in church. Repeat the guidelines every Sunday, especially early in the year when new children have been promoted into children's church. Let them know what's acceptable and what's not.

Having Mom and Dad close can also be a benefit. The

community dynamics of a smaller church tend to keep discipline problems down because parents are often within earshot.

But what if a child is still disruptive? Here are a few ground rules: Be sure that discipline is consistent and fair; give a warning (maybe two); if the disruptive behavior continues, separate the child from the class; if the problem persists, return the child to his or her parents. It won't be a happy time for anyone, but it will likely improve behavior the next week.

Children and Worship

Though both children and adults can worship God, they tend to worship very differently. Adults may want to calmly and reverently praise God, but children want to jump, clap, and yell their praise to God.

Develop a worship experience for children that allows them the active, noisy praise that they love. Children's church is a great time to teach kids to celebrate God. It also shows them how to participate and lead in church.

However, make sure children join in adult worship once in a while. Occasional participation in adult worship services lets children experience and appreciate the reverent praise of most adults. Also, older church members and young children can serve and worship God together. It allows children to learn the traditions of their own faith—to appreciate their church.

Consider what the children in your church need to learn about worship. Then tailor your worship time to suit your children. Whatever path you choose, help your children learn to make worship an important part of their lives.

Chapter Ten

REACHING OUT

"Jesus said, 'Come follow me, and I will make you fish for people' "
(Matthew 4:19).

When Jesus called his disciples, he said they would "fish" for people, and that's a fitting analogy for children's ministry, too. Our job is to fish for children—to find them and to help them begin relationships with God that will last for eternity.

As any fisherman knows, fishing is big business. Multimillion-dollar companies have designed countless gadgets to make finding and catching fish easier. But when it comes right down to it, you only need a few simple things: a stick, some string, and a baited hook. Children's ministry is much the same.

As children's ministers, we want to find new and better programs and resources to minister to children. But we must also remember that outreach is a simple business. We need to find children and tell them about Jesus.

Smaller churches don't need to invest huge amounts of money in outreach. Rather, the best ministry tool that children's workers in small churches can develop is an outreach attitude. Successful outreach occurs when smaller churches learn to be "seeker sensitive."

The concept—though it's nothing new—has been popularized by Willow Creek Community Church, located in the Chicago suburbs. Average Sunday morning attendance at Willow Creek is around 15,000 people. What makes Willow Creek unique is its seeker-sensitive strategy for reaching unchurched people. A small church can't suddenly become a Willow Creek, but any church can address the problems Willow Creek addressed in becoming seeker sensitive.

Many things in the church are confusing and can be easily misunderstood by unchurched people, children and adults alike. The church contributes to misunderstandings through perplexing language and religious traditions. We may chuckle or cringe when children say, "Our Father, who aren't in heaven, Harold be your name," but it's serious. Children need to understand what happens in church. When we become seeker sensitive, we strive to make what happens in church relevant to children's lives.

The seeker-sensitive philosophy also attempts to reach people at every level of spiritual maturity and move them into discipleship opportunities. A smaller church can develop a variety of ministries geared specifically for special interests, ages, or circumstances. In one church, being seeker sensitive toward children might mean developing a program for kids who have nowhere to go after school—helping them with homework and entertaining them until parents get home. In another church, it might mean starting a choir for musically gifted children. Essentially, being seeker sensitive means seeing needs and meeting them.

Evangelistic outreach works well with small groups. I once started meeting with a group of boys who liked to get together and trade baseball cards. Their interest in baseball cards helped them form a tightknit group. It was easy to start a Bible study with them, even though some were not church kids.

Some people are critical of the seeker-sensitive philosophy. They question whether catering to the unchurched will produce church growth in every situation. But we must carefully define our goals. If you consider being seeker sensitive a gimmick to turn your congregation into another

THE BANFORD VALLEY CHURCH STOOPS TO RAW COMMERCIALISM IN ITS ATTEMPT TO INCREASE ATTENDANCE.

Willow Creek, you'll be disappointed. It's not a quick fix for low attendance.

To be seeker sensitive is to be motivated by love—not love for numbers and buildings, but for broken lives and souls. Even a church in the most rural of communities can be sensitive to the unchurched. Such a church may not always pack the pews, but it will see spiritual changes and growth in the lives of individuals.

Think about what Jesus said he had come to do: "The Son of Man came to find lost people and save them" (Luke 19:10). Jesus was seeker sensitive, and Jesus loved children. He sought them out, placed them on his lap, blessed them, and challenged his disciples to become like them.

Smaller churches must listen to children to find out where children are hurting and what they need. Then our children's ministries must devise plans to meet kids' needs.

The rest of this chapter is a collection of ideas for leaders of smaller-church children's ministries who are convinced that their mission is to be seeker sensitive.

Neighborhood Ministry

The smaller church can be particularly effective in neighborhood ministry if it's friendly and approachable. The more interest a church shows in families surrounding the church building, the more user-friendly it will become.

Children can be involved in ministry to their neighborhoods. The eight ideas below connect church children with their neighborhood peers.[1]

● **Host a neighborhood yard sale.** Have church children donate toys, clothing, and household articles. Spend all the proceeds on community outreach projects, such as putting in a basketball court.

● **Offer after-school or evening child care to neighborhood parents.** This could be a weekly or monthly event. Use church teenagers and older children as helpers. Many parents will take advantage of such a service, especially around holidays.

● **Develop a "little brother, little sister" program.** Team church children and neighborhood children together. Or put church families with neighborhood families. Encourage monthly activities together.

● **Hold a monthly birthday party.** Invite the whole neighborhood and celebrate that month's birthday children. Provide cake and ice cream and a small gift for each birthday child. Play games and sing songs.

● **Give away your Christmas tree.** Buy a fresh tree for your church and have children decorate it. About a week before Christmas, give it away to a family without a tree. Give out cookies and sing a few Christmas carols. Be sure to let your congregation know what happened to the tree.

● **Set up a video lending library.** Encourage church members to donate or purchase movies portraying positive Christian values. Make them available for loan to church or neighborhood families. Require a small deposit, then refund it upon return of the tape.

● **Provide free ice water or soft drinks at area functions** (county fairs, parades, yard sales). Have the children prepare and serve it.

● **Hold a Neighborhood Labor Day.** Arrange in advance for small groups of children (with one adult per group) to walk through the neighborhood and pick up trash. You can also offer to help elderly people rake lawns or plant gardens.

People will view the church as an extension of the neighborhood, not as an unapproachable business or religious institution.

Whatever your church's location, your neighborhood holds hundreds of ministry opportunities. To begin finding those opportunities, ask yourself these questions:

• What's the predominant "background" (race, culture, economic status) of the neighborhood surrounding the church building?

• What issues capture the attention of families in this neighborhood (education, safety, crime, poverty)?

• What seems to be the greatest *physical* need of neighborhood families? the greatest *emotional* need?

• When I drive to church, what activities (games, entertainment) do I see neighborhood children participating in?

Once you've identified the situation and the needs of your neighborhood, you're ready to get started. The next step is to brainstorm—as an individual or in a group of interested adults—creative ways to serve your neighborhood. Ask: What can your church do to catch the attention of neighborhood children? Maybe it's putting up a basketball hoop or inviting in-line skating on your parking lot. Perhaps it's setting up a small petting zoo or providing cold drinks on hot summer days.

Examine how each of these activities could minister to the children of your neighborhood. Then choose one or two that you decide would meet needs and be most effective in reaching unchurched children. Keep the other ideas on record for later development. Find leaders to get these programs started, and involve your own church's children in the outreach in whatever roles they can serve. When problems come up, don't give up easily. Remember that your goal is to help children know, love, and serve Jesus.

Family Ministry

One way to help children grow spiritually is through ministry to the whole family. The smaller church has tremendous strengths when it comes to "family" ministry because keeping families together for activities is more natural with smaller numbers of people.

You can use this natural focus to tremendous advantage in your community. The opportunities are endless, and most are inexpensive. One small church developed monthly YMCA gym and pool nights for families. You can also host family bowling nights, family roller-skating parties, or family pizza blasts.

Schedule times for families to study and grow together. Make your midweek program a family Bible study or try keeping families together in an intergenerational Sunday school. Encourage church families to invite neighborhood families to join them for worship services. Have family members provide special music together or take on service projects together. You might have a family fold bulletins or make flower arrangements for the sanctuary. Instead of having ushers or couples greet worshipers at the door, have families greet them.

Christian Education

Even parents who aren't regular church attenders often recognize the importance of religious education for their children. Christian education—through day care, preschools, and Christian schools—has grown dramatically within the last decade. All of these can be effective tools for reaching neighborhood families and bringing them to the church.

Christian Day Care

As more and more women have moved into the work force, the need for day care has mushroomed. Many small churches can easily provide this care for neighborhood families. In fact, some smaller churches have discovered that a church day care ministry is a double blessing: It provides the potential for a small profit and it exposes unchurched families to the ministries of the church.

Be sure to check out all the legal issues before launching a day care program. Governmental restrictions continue to tighten. Most states now require licensing and some also require day care facilities to meet special building codes. Creating a day care center that's up to code can be expensive, and many small churches give up. But other affordable, appropriate space may be available. One small church rents space in a busy strip mall and offers tenants and shoppers long-term or short-term child care. Another congregation advertises listings of church members who provide licensed home day care.

Don't expect your day care program to immediately add lots of income to your children's ministry. Start-up costs can be high. Few day care centers turn a profit before their third year. One solution is to develop strategies to meet start-up costs before you open for business. One church of 75 people discovered it could break even with special fund-raisers run by the parents who used the day care. Though finances may initially be a problem, churches that develop day care programs often reap the reward as new families are attracted to the church.

Christian Preschool

Many churches have found Christian preschool to be a terrific way to serve the community and bring people into the church. However, as with Christian day care, bringing a facility up to local building codes can be expensive. Older buildings will require the most changes. But newer buildings—especially those built in the last ten years—may require few changes.

One benefit of preschool programming is its half-day structure. A church can offer both morning and afternoon classes using the same staff, and lots of children can be involved. Higher enrollments mean better use of the facility and a greater likelihood of breaking even financially.

In many states, preschool teachers need not be certified instructors. This is both positive and negative. It provides a greater pool of teachers from which to draw; however, lack of certification can also tempt churches to forego crucial background checks. A small church cannot afford to risk a lawsuit—always check out potential child care workers *thoroughly.*

Do your homework before you decide to open a preschool. Find out what your state requires. Some states' requirements are fairly lax, while other states create bureaucratic nightmares. Furthermore, if other Christian preschools already exist in your area, drawing new families may be difficult. Talk to other churches that operate Christian preschools. Do they have annual waiting lists? If not, there may not be a need.

Christian Schools

Opening a Christian school is an option you may consider beyond your church's abilities. But some small churches make it work. Bountiful Christian Church, a small congregation in northern Utah, has met with incredible success with its school. The church is serious about its commitment to its preschool and elementary school—the church bylaws state that the church cannot exist without the school and vice versa. It's a true partnership.

Almost 100 children, toddlers through sixth grade, attend annually. That's more than twice the church's Sunday attendance, and school enrollment climbs each year. Located in the heart of Mormon country, the school draws children from all different denominations and even non-Christian families.

The facilities are small yet modern, including a house next to the church and a modular unit. The school is run by a single administrator who's also the church's pastor. The church employs four full-time, certified teachers for kindergarten through sixth grade, three full-time and six part-time instructors for the preschool, and a part-time secretary. One additional part-time secretary donates her time.

Seventy percent of the school's operating cost (mortgage, utilities, salaries, and insurance) is covered by tuition. The school uses fund-raisers to meet the rest of the costs, including property and building improvements. A Bowl-a-Thon each fall nets around $10,000 (children enlist sponsors and bowl for donated prizes from area shopping centers). A pizza drive in which schoolchildren both sell and make the pizzas will earn $3.50 per pizza for the school. And a "recycling and receipt" competition between several Salt Lake City area nonprofit organizations will reap another $1,400.

To help with labor costs, the school requires parents to volunteer a minimum of two hours a month to the school or be billed for unserved hours. All families understand this financial policy prior to their children's acceptance into the school. Volunteers do a variety of jobs. They mow grass, paint, lead reading groups, bake cookies, and organize fund-raisers.

The school also depends on special gifts and donations—such as the 12×40-foot mobile office donated recently—and is careful with the income. "We use business principles based on faith," states the pastor and administrator. The school's tuition is lower than that at other private Christian schools in the area, the school has a reputation for excellent education, and the children's ministry of that church touches kids' lives every day of the week!

Because of the school's influence, Bountiful Christian Church has also grown. Five new families joined the congregation last year alone. This church is an example of a small church that refuses to be limited by its size.

Your church may be able to enjoy the same kind of ministry. Seek what God has for your church. Maybe your church will offer a tremendous after-school program or an excellent VBS. Maybe you'll revamp your Sunday school into a dynamic family-based ministry. Whatever you do, seek God's vision, find out what the children in your church and your area need, and make it happen.

A Final Word

The smaller church is a wonderful place packed with opportunity. Your charge is to determine your opportunities and to turn those opportunities into a dynamic ministry to help children know and love God.

Maybe you're still wondering where to start. That's OK. Take some time to evaluate where your church is and where you want it to be. Include others in developing a vision of what can happen in your church's children's ministry. Then get planning and get started! The final word in this discussion does not belong to me.

It really belongs to you.

---

1. Many of these ideas have been adapted from Anthony Campolo, *Ideas for Social Action* (Grand Rapids, MI: Zondervan/Youth Specialties, 1983), 36-74.

RECOMMENDED RESOURCES

(Note: Although all the resources listed here are helpful in their own ways, the author and Group Publishing do not necessarily agree with or endorse all ideas presented in all of these resources.)

- *Adventures in Odyssey* video series. Colorado Springs, CO: Focus on the Family Films. Animated stories that present Christian principles through entertainment.
- Barna, George. *The Power of Vision: How You Can Capture & Apply God's Vision for Your Ministry.* Ventura, CA: Regal Books, 1992.
- CHILDREN'S MINISTRY Magazine. Loveland, CO: Group Publishing.
- Cionca, John R. *Solving Church Education's Ten Toughest Problems.* Wheaton, IL: Scripture Press Publications, 1990.
- Daniel, Eleanor. *ABCs of VBS.* Cincinnati: Standard Publishing, 1994.
- Dudley, Carl S. *Making the Small Church Effective.* Nashville, TN: Abingdon Press, 1978.
- *Fun-to-Learn Bible Lessons.* Loveland, CO: Group Publishing, 1993. A series of books with active lessons for children in preschool through sixth grade.
- Group's Hands-On Bible Curriculum™. Loveland, CO: Group Publishing. Quarterly Sunday school curriculum utilizing active and interactive learning. Consists of a teachers guide and a Learning Lab® box filled with creative classroom learning gizmos. Available for preschool through sixth-grade classes.
- Group's MinistryNet™ computer on-line service. Loveland, CO: Group Publishing, 1995. An on-line service connecting children's workers around the country with one another and with ministry resources.

- *Group's Preschool Teacher Training* video training series. Loveland, CO: Group Publishing, 1995.
- Healy, Jane M. *How to Have Intelligent & Creative Conversations With Your Kids.* New York: Doubleday, 1994.
- Healy, Jane M. *Your Child's Growing Mind: A Guide to Learning & Brain Development.* New York: Doubleday, 1994.
- Keffer, Lois. *Clip & Tell Bible Stories.* Loveland, CO: Group Publishing, 1995.
- Keffer, Lois and Jennifer Root Wilger, eds. *Interactive Bible Stories for Children.* Loveland, CO: Group Publishing, 1994. A series of books that utilize interactive storytelling techniques to relate Old and New Testament Bible stories.
- Keffer, Lois. *Sunday School Specials.* Loveland, CO: Group Publishing, 1992. A series of books with creative lessons for multi-age groups of children.
- Kohl, Mary Ann. *Preschool Art: It's the Process, Not the Product.* Beltsville, MD: Gryphon House, 1994.
- LeBar, Lois E. *Education That Is Christian.* Wheaton, IL: Scripture Press Publications, 1989.
- Lingo, Susan. *Instant Games for Children's Ministry.* Loveland, CO: Group Publishing, 1995.
- Rowland, Beth, ed. *Esteem-Builders for Children's Ministry.* Loveland, CO: Group Publishing, 1992.
- Rowland, Beth, ed. *Quick Games for Children's Ministry.* Loveland, CO: Group Publishing, 1992.
- Roehlkepartain, Eugene C. *The Teaching Church: Moving Christian Education to Center Stage.* Nashville, TN: Abingdon Press, 1993.
- Roehlkepartain, Jolene L., ed. *Children's Ministry That Works!* Loveland, CO: Group Publishing, 1991.
- Roehlkepartain, Jolene L. *Fidget Busters: One Hundred One Quick Attention-Getters for Children's Ministry.* Loveland, CO: Group Publishing, 1992.
- Roehlkepartain, Jolene L. *101 Creative Worship Ideas for Children's Church.* Loveland, CO: Group Publishing, 1995.
- Richards, Lawrence O. *Children's Ministry: Nursing Faith Within the Family of God.* Grand Rapids, MI: Zondervan Publishing, 1988.

● Schaller, Lyle E. *The Small Church Is Different.* Nashville, TN: Abingdon Press, 1982.

● Schultz, Thom and Joani. *Why Nobody Learns Much of Anything at Church: And How to Fix It.* Loveland, CO: Group Publishing, 1993.

● *Teaching Children in the Church* video training series. Loveland, CO: Group Publishing, 1992.

● Tobias, Cynthia U. *The Way They Learn.* Colorado Springs: Focus on the Family Publishing, 1994.

● Towns, Elmer L. *Ten Sunday Schools That Dared to Change: How Churches Are Changing Paradigms to Reach a New Generation.* Ventura, CA: Regal Books, 1993.

● Wilger, Jennifer R., ed. *Group's Best-Ever Children's Ministry Clip Art.* Loveland, CO: Group Publishing, 1994.

● Yount, Christine. *Big Action Bible Skits.* Loveland, CO: Group Publishing, 1995.

● Yount, Christine, ed. *Helping Children Know God.* Loveland, CO: Group Publishing, 1995.

Evaluation of *Children's Ministry Guide for Smaller Churches*

Please help Group Publishing, Inc., continue providing innovative and usable resources for ministry by taking a moment to fill out and send us this evaluation. Thanks!

● ● ●

1. As a whole, this book has been (circle one)

Not much help   Very helpful

1   2   3   4   5   6   7   8   9   10

2. The things I liked best about this book were...

3. This book could be improved by...

4. One thing I'll do differently because of this book is...

5. Optional Information:

Name _____

Street Address _____

City _____ State_____ Zip_____

Phone Number _____ Date_____

TEACH YOUR PRESCHOOLERS AS JESUS TAUGHT... WITH GROUP'S *HANDS-ON BIBLE CURRICULUM*™

Hands-On Bible Curriculum™ **for preschoolers** helps your preschoolers learn e way they learn best—by touching, exploring, and discovering. With active learning, eschoolers love learning about the Bible, and they really remember what they learn.

Because small children learn best through repetition, Preschoolers and Pre-K & K II learn one important point per lesson, and Toddlers & 2s will learn one point each onth with **Hands-On Bible Curriculum**. These important lessons will stick with em and comfort them during their daily lives. Your children will learn God is our end, who Jesus is, and we can always trust Jesus.

The **Learning Lab**® is packed with age-appropriate learning tools for fun, faith-ilding lessons. Toddlers & 2s explore big **Interactive StoryBoards**™ with enticing tures that toddlers love to touch. **Bible Big Books**™ captivate Preschoolers and -K & K while teaching them important Bible lessons. With **Jumbo Bible Puzzles**™ d involving **Learning Mats**™, your children will see, touch, and explore their Bible ries. Each quarter there's a brand new collection of supplies to keep your lessons sh and involving.

Fuzzy, age-appropriate hand puppets are also available to add to the learning perience. These child-friendly puppets help you teach each lesson with scripts ovided in the **Teachers Guide**. Cuddles the Lamb, Whiskers the Mouse, and ckets the Kangaroo turn each lesson into an interactive and entertaining learning perience.

Just order one **Learning Lab** and one **Teachers Guide** for each age level, add a v common classroom supplies, and presto—you have everything you need to build th in your children. **No student books required!**

Hands-On Bible Curriculum is also available for grades 1–6.

BRING THE BIBLE TO LIFE FOR YOUR 1ST THROUGH 6TH GRADERS WITH GROUP'S *HANDS-ON BIBLE CURRICULUM*™

Group's **Hands-On Bible Curriculum**™ will help you teach the Bible in a radical new way. It's based on Active Learning—the same teaching method Jesus used.

In each lesson, students will participate in exciting and memorable learning experiences using fascinating gadgets and gizmos you've not seen with any other curriculum. Your elementary students will discover biblical truths and <u>remember</u> what they learn because they're <u>doing</u> instead of just listening

You'll save time and money too!

While students are learning more, you'll be working less—simply follow the quick and easy instructions in the **Teachers Guide**. You'll get tons of material for an energy-packed 35-60 minute lesson. In addition to the easy-to-use **Teachers Guide**, you'll get all the essential teaching materials you need in a ready-to-use **Learning Lab**®. Plus, you'll SAVE BIG over other curriculum programs that require you to buy expensive separate student books—all student handouts in Group's **Hands-On Bible Curriculum** are photocopiable!

Challenging topics each quarter keep your kids coming back!

Group's **Hands-On Bible Curriculum** covers topics that matter to your kids and teaches them the Bible with integrity. Switching topics every month keeps your 1st through 6th graders enthused and coming back for more. The full two-year program will help your kids make God-pleasing decisions, recognize their God-given potential, and seek to grow as Christians.

Take the boredom out of Sunday school, children's church, and midweek meetings for your elementary students. Make your job easier and more rewarding with no-fail lessons that are ready in a flash. Order Group's **Hands-On Bible Curriculum** for your 1st through 6th graders today.

Hands-On Bible Curriculum is also available for Toddlers & 2s, Preschool, and Pre-K and K

INNOVATIVE RESOURCES FOR
YOUR CHILDREN'S MINISTRY

g Action Bible Skits

ristine Yount

At last—drama that's both exciting *and* easy! Using eight full-color overhead ¡nsparencies and ten skits, your elementary children will learn about the Bible as ¿y act out favorite Old Testament Bible stories—without expensive scenery and ⸱s. Simply shine the appropriate overhead on the wall and presto—instant staging!

Encourage learning by helping your children experience Bible stories...and have ¬ at the same time. Five- to 10-minute skits include...

- •Adam and Eve,
- •Noah and the Ark,
- •Moses and the Exodus,
- •Jonah and the Big Fish, and more!

⸱N 1-55945-258-7

⸱lping Children Know God

A must for anyone who wants to help elementary-age children understand ⸱ecific attributes of God. Here's active learning at its best—program ideas appeal to ⸱ five senses and include suggestions for use in and out of the classroom. You'll help ⸱ildren discover...

- •God is loving
- •God is faithful
- •God is all-knowing
- •God is everywhere...and more!

With 140 ideas for helping children know God, this book will be a part of your ⸱son planning week after week.

⸱N 1-55945-605-1

⸱1 Creative Worship Ideas for Children's Church

ene Roehlkepartain

Get your children excited about God with over 100 new, creative ideas for ⸱ildren's worship. Each idea is easy to use and works for children's church, Sunday ⸱hool, or any place children are gathered to worship God.

You'll discover ideas for...

- •prayers
- •devotions
- •puppet scripts
- •object lessons
- •Bible stories
- •holidays, and more!

Written by children's ministry veteran Jolene Roehlkepartain, this book is jam ⸱cked with creative ideas that will help you lead your children in worship meetings ⸱at are exciting and meaningful.

⸱N 1-55945-601-9

Order today from your local Christian bookstore, or write:
Group Publishing, Box 485, Loveland, CO 80539.